P9-DBS-517

John

and

His Witness

Zacchaeus Studies: New Testament

General Editor: Mary Ann Getty

John

and

His Witness

by
Raymond F. Collins

A Michael Glazier Book
THE LITURGICAL PRESS
Collegeville, Minnesota

A Michael Glazier Book published by The Liturgical Press.

Cover by Don Bruno.

Copyright © 1991 by The Order of St. Benedict, Inc., Collegeville, Minnesota. All rights reserved. No part of this book may be reproduced in any form or by any means, electronic or mechanical, including photocopying, recording, taping, or any retrieval system, without the written permission of The Liturgical Press, Collegeville, Minnesota 56321. Printed in the United States of America.

1   2   3   4   5   6   7   8   9

Library of Congress Cataloging-in-Publication Data

Collins, Raymond F., 1935–
    John and his witness / by Raymond F. Collins.
        p.   cm.
    Includes bibliographical references and indexes.
    ISBN 0-8146-5670-6
    1. Bible. N.T. John—Criticism, interpretation, etc. 2. Witness bearing (Christianity) in the Bible. I. Title.
    BS2615.6.W54C65   1991   90-24727
    226.5'06—dc20   CIP

To J. K.
through whom the Father
sustained a vision.

CONTENTS

Editor's Note

Zacchaeus Studies provide concise, readable and relatively inexpensive scholarly studies on particular aspects of scripture and theology. The New Testament section of the series presents studies dealing with focal or debated questions; and the volumes focus on specific texts or particular themes of current interest in biblical interpretation. Specialists have their professional journals and other forums where they discuss matters of mutual concern, exchange ideas and further contemporary trends of research; and some of their work on contemporary biblical research is now made accessible for students and others in *Zacchaeus Studies*.

The authors in this series share their own scholarship in nontechnical language, in the areas of their expertise and interest. These writers stand with the best in current biblical scholarship in the English-speaking world. Since most of them are teachers, they are accustomed to presenting difficult material in comprehensible form without compromising a high level of critical judgment and analysis.

The works of this series are ecumenical in content and purpose and cross credal boundaries. They are designed to augment formal and informal biblical study and discussion. Hopefully they will also serve as texts to enhance and supplement seminary, university and college classes. The series will also aid Bible study groups, adult education and parish religious education classes to develop intelligent, versatile and challenging programs for those they serve.

Mary Ann Getty
New Testament Editor

1

John

After the magnificent prologue (John 1:1-18), which places the subject of the Fourth Gospel's narrative in the broadest possible context of time and space, the evangelist begins his account in earnest when he writes, "And this is the testimony of John" (John 1:19).

John 1: 19-23

This opening seems to suggest that the evangelist's readers are about to look in upon a courtroom drama. The initial impression is not far off target. Immediately the evangelist presents John as the subject of a formal inquiry. "The Jews," presumably some sort of officialdom, have sent a delegation to query John. The delegation consists of priests and Levites, jointly responsible for the care of the Temple in Jerusalem. Their first question is apparently innocent enough. They ask, "Who are you?", a not unlikely request for identification as the process begins. John's response is, however, not quite innocent. Rather than identify himself, he responds by formally stating, almost swearing, in fact, who he is not. His confession is that he is not the Christ.

Thereupon the official delegation presses the issue of the witness' identification. Additional questions flow rapidly from their lips. "Are you Elijah?" "Are you the prophet?" To each of these queries the witness responds negatively. So, again, and seemingly in a state of frustration, the interrogators ask, "Who are you?" Thus pressed, the witness ironically replies in words taken from the biblical prophet Isaiah: "I am the voice of one crying in the wilderness, 'Make straight the way of the Lord' " (Isa 40:3).

In most courtroom scenes the identification of the witness is a relatively routine matter, but this is not the case of the witness named John. He is more concerned with saying who he is not—a kind of negative identification—than in saying who he is. When finally he identifies himself, his self-identity is revealed to be that of "the voice."

The posture of the witness who is so reluctant to identify himself contributes to the drama about to unfold. The reader's curiosity has been whetted from the outset. One would like to know who this Christ is who John is not. And if John is only a voice, what has he to say? These are the kinds of questions that arise within the reader's mind as he or she contemplates the first scene in the Johannine drama.

The confrontation between John and the delegation of interrogators has been carefully staged by the evangelist. A contemporary reader familiar with the other New Testament Gospels (Matthew, Mark, and Luke) realizes that the story of John's interrogation does not appear in these Synoptic texts; however, he or she may know that messianic speculation was rife in first century Palestine. Over the course of several decades and in various Jewish circles, questions had been raised about the identity of the Christ, a transliteration of the Greek equivalent of the Hebrew word "messiah,"[1] the anointed one, the one smeared with oil.

Questions abounded as to who the Christ might be. There was also speculation in the air about the return of some other long-awaited end-time figures. Some of this speculation is reflected in the Synoptic Gospels, as for instance in the Lukan account of the popular enthusiasm about John (Luke 3:15) and his story of Herod's anxiety after the death of John (Luke 9:7-9). Speculation of this sort serves as the real-life background to the question addressed to Jesus by John's disciples at John's own request (Matt 11:2-6; Luke 7:18-23) as well as to the various responses given when Jesus asks his disciples what people are saying about him (Matt 16:13-16; Mark 8:27-29; Luke 9:18-20).

[1] Cf. John 1:41.

Since kings were commonly anointed, the Christ, for whose appearance many first-century Jews were waiting, was truly a royal figure. He was expected to be an ideal king, much in the mold of David, father of kings. As David had achieved hegemony over the land of Israel and had unified the separate tribes, the awaited king was expected to restore Jewish control over the land of Palestine and reunite the Jews then in dispersion. His appearance was to be an effective sign of the reign of God, for then the theocracy of Israel would be fully and finally established.

There was also a popular view, supported by some of those professionally competent in biblical lore,[2] that the prophet Elijah would return as the herald of the day of the Lord. The biblical tradition had told the story of Elijah's having been taken up to heaven in a whirlwind while riding in a fiery chariot (2 Kgs 2:1, 11-12; Sir 48:1, 9, 12). The prophet Malachi had spoken of a messenger who would come to prepare the day of the Lord (Mal 3:1-3), and a later editor of his work added a note to the effect that this messenger was to be Elijah (Mal 4:5-6). Subsequently[3] —and to this day—many pious Jews waited for the return of Elijah.

Still other Jews were anxiously awaiting the appearance of an end-time prophetic figure. From time immemorial prophets had arisen to announce the mighty interventions of Yahweh in human history. According to the Jewish philosopher Philo of Alexandria, Moses himself was "everywhere celebrated as a prophet" *(Quis rerum,* 262). According to the *Teaching of Markah,* a third- or fourth-century Samaritan text, Moses was "the prophet whose prophethood is a treasure which will not be removed from him as long as the world lasts" *(Memar Markah,* VI, 9). Responding to the announcement of a prophet to come in Deuteronomy 18:15, 18, the Samaritans believed that Moses himself would come back to deliver Israel.[4]

---

[2]Cf. Matthew 17:10; Mark 9:11.

[3]See the commentary in the *Mishnah,* Eduyoth, 8, 7.

[4]See *Memar Markah,* III, 3.

John categorically denies that he is Moses *redivivus* or any other kind of end-time prophet like unto Moses,[5] just as he has categorically denied that he is Elijah returned to earth or the long-awaited Christ. John virtually swears that he is not to be identified with any of the well-known end-time characters expected by the adherents to the various strains of first-century Judaism. At most he is to be identified with "the voice" of which the Deutero-Isaiah had written.

John 1:24-28

Nonetheless the interrogation continues. In a paragraph that appears to be a literary doublet of the preceding interrogation, John is queried as to why he is baptizing. The evangelist observes that the inquisitors have been sent by a group belonging to the Pharisees, essentially Jews devoted to the strict observance of the Mosaic Law. By portraying John as testifying under pressure before the Pharisees as well as before a delegation of priests and Levites, the evangelist provides his readers with an image of John who not only refuses to identify himself with any of the awaited eschatological figures, but as one who also testifies before the delegates of the whole Jewish world.[6]

Ancient Jewish literary sources did not provide any indication that either the Christ, an Elijah or Moses *redivivus,* or any future prophet like Moses was expected to do any baptizing. Thus the question addressed to John by this delegation of interrogators is that of his authority. By what authority does John baptize? That kind of question was apparently raised in Jewish and early Christian circles, undoubtedly even in Jerusalem itself.[7] Once again, however, John seems to evade the question posed by his interrogators. Only enigmatically does he respond to their query. Of himself, the voice acknowledges only that he baptizes with

---

[5]See, among the Qumran texts, 1QS 9:11.

[6]See the corresponding use of the phrase "Pharisees and Sadducees" in the Gospel of Matthew (Matt 3:7; 16:1, 6, 11, 12). The Sadducees represented the priestly sect in first-century Judaism.

[7]See Matthew 21:23-26; Mark 11:27-32; Luke 20:1-6.

water. Yet he goes on to say that there "stands among you one whom you do not know, even he who comes after me, the thong of whose sandal I am not worthy to untie" (John 1:27-28).

John seems to be here making reference to a Jewish tradition according to which the Messiah would remain relatively obscure until the moment of his presentation to Israel—by Elijah, according to the most common understanding.[8] His earlier emphatic statement, "*I* (the use of the pronoun *egō* is unnecessary in Greek) am not the Christ," had implied that nonetheless the Christ was somewhere about. Now John implies that the Christ is hidden, that the difference of status between himself and the hidden one is greater than that which exists between a revered master and his student.

An Aside

The reader familiar with the story of John the Baptist according to the Synoptic tradition (Matt 3:1-17; Mark 1:2-11; Luke 3:1-20) will surely note that the fourth evangelist has thus far placed relatively little emphasis upon the fact that John is one who baptizes. John's baptismal activity serves only as the subject of the interrogation. In fact, the fourth evangelist does not even present John as a prophetic figure who proclaims the need for repentance as the kingdom of God is about to draw near. Rather, he is concerned with establishing John's identity as "the voice" who has something to say.

This self-identification, which the evangelist places on the very lips of John, is one of the features that distinguishes the fourth evangelist's characterization of John from that of the Synoptic authors. In each of their works, the Isaian text "the voice of one crying in the wilderness: Prepare the way of the Lord" (Isa 40:3) is introduced into the Gospel narrative under the guise of a commentary by the evangelist (Matt 3:3; Mark 1:3; Luke 3:4). In the Fourth Gospel, however, it is John himself who attributes to himself the role of the voice. The evangelist wants his John to "speak for himself."

[8]See Justin, *Dialogue with Trypho* 8, 4, 49, 110; PG 6, 493.

Undoubtedly the evangelist expects his contemporary readers to be generally familiar with the story of John. That is why he can introduce him simply by calling him "John." Those same readers would have been struck by the evangelist's seeming lack of interest in John's baptizing, a disinterest attested to by the fact that he attributes to John neither the title "Baptist," so dear to Matthew (Matt 3:1) and subsequent Christian tradition, nor the descriptive phrase "the baptizer," to be found in Mark (Mark 1:4).

The evangelist's story of John is the evangelist's own story. He has his own way of describing John and exerts considerable literary skill in sharing his vision of John with his readers. It is not only that the double interrogation does not appear in the earlier Gospels or that the evangelist's characterization of John is uniquely his that highlights the fact that the evangelist is telling his own story. There is, in addition, the language and literary style of the evangelist's account.[9] One can take note of the dialogue, the use of questions, and the buildup of dramatic little scenes, characteristic of the fourth evangelist's entire narrative. He has a flair for dramatic presentation, accentuated by careful adherence to the "rule of two"—with no more than two speakers appearing in any one scene. This technique allows each little scene to have its own focus.

The courtroom-like drama of the two-phase interrogation of John certainly provides a dramatic atmosphere as the evangelist begins his narrative. His language really does smack of the courtroom. He writes of testimony *(marturia,* v. 19), confession *(homologeō,* twice in v. 20), and denial *(arneomai,* v. 20). He writes of questioning *(erōtaō,* vv. 19, 21, 25) and answering *(apokrinomai,* vv. 21, 26; *apokrisis,* v. 22) and of those who have been sent *(apostellō,* vv. 19, 22, 24).

The juridical language that so vividly colors the first scenario is characteristic of the entire narrative. The language of the court-

---

[9]On the characteristic features of the evangelist's style, See M.-E. Boismard and A. Lamouille, *Synopse des quatre évangiles en français,* 3: *L'évangile de Jean* (Paris: Cerf, 1977) 491–531 and Frans Neirynck, *Jean et les Synoptiques: Examen critique de l'exégèse de M.-E. Boismard* (Bibliotheca Ephemeridum Theologicarum Lovaniensium, 49; Louvain: University Press, 1979) 45–66.

room runs throughout the story, which contains a fairly large dose
of blatantly legal terminology. Words such as accuse *(katēgoreō)*[10]
and convict *(elegchō),*[11] defender *(paraklētos),*[12] judgment *(kri-sis)*[13] and judge *(krinō),*[14] provide verve and color for the tale the
evangelist unfolds.

The most striking example of the evangelist's choice of language
that belongs to the forensic register is the word "testimony" *(mar-turia),* the term with which the present dramatic little scene opens,
and the related verb *martureō,* which means "to testify" or "to
bear witness."[15] "Testimony" *(marturia)* occurs fourteen times
in the Fourth Gospel,[16] while the cognate verb "to testify" *(mar-tureō)* occurs thirty-three times.[17]

The fourth evangelist's use of the language of the courtroom
sharply distinguishes his story from those of the earlier evangelists,
Matthew, Mark, and Luke. These Gospel writers seldom use terms
like "testimony"[18] and "to testify."[19] Instead, they seem to pre-fer such terms as "to proclaim" *(kērussō)* or "to announce the
good news" *(euaggelizomai).*

Undoubtedly, the fourth evangelist's inclination to use legal lan-guage as frequently as he does is due to the circumstances in which
his Gospel was written. Although it is difficult to determine the

[10]John 5:45; 8:6.

[11]John 3:20; 8:46; 16:8.

[12]John 14:16, 26; 15:26; 16:7.

[13]John 3:19; 5:22, 24, 27, 29, 30; 7:24; 8:16; 12:31; 16:8, 11.

[14]John 3:17, 18 (twice); 5:22, 30; 7:24 (twice), 51; 8:15 (twice), 16, 26, 50; 12:47 (twice), 48 (twice); 16:11; 18:31. In some of these passages the verb *krinō* is translated "condemn" in some versions, e.g., RSV, John 3:17-18.

[15]A major study of the motif has been made by Johannes Beutler. See J. Beutler, *Mar-tyria: Traditionsgeschichtliche Untersuchungen zum Zeugnisthema bei Johannes* (Frankfurter theologische Studien, 10; Frankfurt, Knecht, 1972).

[16]John 1:7, 19; 3:11, 32, 33; 5:31, 32, 34, 36; 8:13, 14, 17; 19:35; 21:24.

[17]John 1:7, 8, 15, 32, 34; 2:25; 3:11, 26, 28, 32; 4:39, 44; 5:31, 32 (twice), 33, 36, 37, 39; 7:7; 8:13, 14, 18 (twice); 10:25; 12:17; 13:21; 15:26, 27; 18:23, 37; 19:35; 21:24.

[18]The noun does not occur at all in Matthew's Gospel. It is to be found just three times in Mark (14:55, 56, 59) and once in Luke (22:71). All four of these instances occur in the story of Jesus' trial.

[19]The verb does not occur in Mark. It is found once in Matthew (23:31) and once in Luke (4:22).

date of composition of the Fourth Gospel with any precision—a difficulty exacerbated by the fact that the Fourth Gospel we now possess represents an edited version of an earlier text, which in turn may well have been an edited version of a still earlier text— most scholars are convinced that the Fourth Gospel was composed in the mid- to late nineties, that is, just before the turn of the first Christian century.

By that time, Christians living in Jewish communities had experienced the pain of separation from their fellow Jews. Not only had Christians become aware that their acknowledgment of Jesus as Messiah made them a distinct entity within the ethnic Jewish community, but Jesus-confessors were also looked upon with no little suspicion by the Jewish community itself. The times were, after all, difficult ones for faithful Jews. For centuries they had not enjoyed hegemony over the land which they revered as God's gift and promise to them.[20] In the siege of Jerusalem (A.D. 70) the Temple itself had been destroyed. What remained as a symbol of their ethnic and religious identity was their tradition, embodied in the Scriptures and the synagogue service, which focused on the reading of the Law.

After the destruction of Jerusalem a group of Pharisaic Jews, students of the Law, gathered together in Jabneh. Circumstances dictated that they do all within their power to ensure the vitality and the purity of the Jewish tradition. With renewed vigor these Pharisees, who had always been concerned with the faithful interpretation and observance of the Law, dedicated themselves to the task at hand. From their sessions would eventually emerge a canon of Jewish Scriptures, but they were also concerned about the purity of their prayer and the integrity of their gatherings.

A tradition ascribed to the great rabbi Gamaliel said that "Every day a man should say the eighteen benedictions."[21] In its commentary upon this bit of rabbinic lore, the Talmud inquired "To what do these eighteen benedictions correspond?" After passing

---

[20]See Walter Brueggemann, *The Land: Place as Gift, Promise and Challenge in Biblical Faith.* (Overtures to Bible Theology; Philadelphia: Fortress, 1977).

[21]Mishnah, tractate *Berakoth,* 4, 3.

a series of responses in review, the Talmud raised another question: "These eighteen are really nineteen?" In response,

> R. Levi said: "The benediction relating to the *Minim* was instituted in Jabneh. To what was it meant to correspond? . . . Our Rabbis taught: Simeon ha-Pakuli[22] arranged the eighteen benedictions in order before Rabban Gamaliel in Jabneh. Said Rabban Gamaliel to the Sages: Can any one among you frame a benediction relating to the *Minim?* Samuel the Lesser arose and composed it. The next year he forgot it and he tried for two or three hours to recall it, and they did not remove him. Why did they not remove him seeing that Rab Judah has said in the name of Rab: If a reader made a mistake in any of the other benedictions, they do not remove him, but if in the benediction of the *Minim,* he is removed, because we suspect him of being a *Min?*—Samuel the Lesser is different, because he composed it.[23]

The benediction composed by Samuel was originally appended to the list of eighteen benedictions compiled during Gamaliel's tenure at the head of the academy at Jabneh (ca. A.D. 80-115), but at the present time it is twelfth in order among the eighteen benedictions. Apparently "the benediction" was a type of curse, denouncing the *Minim,* that is, the "slanderers" or "heretics." Scholars think that the benediction was directed, at least to a large extent, against Christians. Unable in conscience to denounce themselves, they would avoid the utterance of the benediction against the *Minim* and would be expelled from the synagogue,[24] a fate which would have befallen the forgetful Samuel himself were it not for the fact that he had composed that very benediction.

The formulation of this famous twelfth benediction is a striking example of the scrutiny to which the Jewish Christians of the

---

[22]An epithet which may mean "the cotton dealer."

[23]Babylonian Talmud, tractate *Berakoth* 28b-29a, quoted according to the translation of Maurice Simon (London: Socino, 1960).

[24]See J. Louis Martyn, *History and Theology in the Fourth Gospel,* 2nd ed. (Nashville: Abingdon, 1979) 50-62.

evangelist's day were apparently subject because of their confession of Jesus as the Christ. It is quite likely that real-life controversies between the members of the Johannine circle[25] and the defenders of Jewish orthodoxy form the background for passages such as John 9:22: "They feared the Jews, for the Jews had already agreed that if anyone should confess him to be Christ, he was to be put out of the synagogue"; John 12:42: "Many even of the authorities believed in him, but for fear of the Pharisees they did not confess it, lest they should be put out of the synagogue"; and John 15:26–16:2: "When the Counsellor comes, whom I shall send to you from the Father . . . he will bear witness to me; and you also are witnesses, because you have been with me from the beginning. I have said all this to you to keep you from falling away. They will put you out of the synagogues." Similarly, the existence of local controversies with the proponents of Jewish orthodoxy probably explains why the Fourth Gospel fairly breathes the atmosphere of the courtroom.

John the Witness

The first witness cited by the evangelist is John. Undoubtedly the evangelist begins his Gospel story with the figure of John because Christian tradition generally saw John as one whose ministry, almost immediately preceding that of Jesus, effectively prepared the way for Jesus' own ministry.[26] Nevertheless the evangelist's characterization of John as a witness is particularly sharp. By John's own testimony, he is only a "voice."

A contemporary reader of the Fourth Gospel cannot overlook the evangelist's finely tuned portrayal of John as a witness. This reader is well aware that the evangelist omits from his initial

---

[25]The expression is taken from the title of Oscar Cullmann's work, *The Johannine Circle* (Philadelphia: Westminster, 1976). In similar fashion Raymond Brown has called the group of Christians from which the Fourth Gospel emerged "the community of the beloved disciple" *(The Community of the Beloved Disciple: The Life, Loves, and Hates of an Individual Church in New Testament Times*, New York: Paulist, 1979).

[26]See Matthew 17:10-13 and Acts 13:24-25 as well as Matthew 3:1-12; Mark 1:2-8; Luke 3:1-20; and the Lukan infancy narrative (Luke 1-2).

presentation of John virtually every reference to his actually baptizing. He likewise passes over in silence not only that John's baptism is for the remission of sins but also that John preaches a baptism of repentance.[27]

One who reads the Gospel in its present format, beginning, that is, from the first verse of the prologue, is also aware that John has already been introduced to the reader as of John 1:6-8: "There was a man sent from God, whose name was John. He came for testimony, to bear witness to the light, that all might believe through him. He was not the light, but came to bear witness to the light." These prose verses interrupt the hitherto poetic structure of the prologue, leading some authors to opine that they might have formed the beginning of the Gospel narrative at some less-than-final edition. Certainly the phrase "there was a man . . . *(egeneto anthrōpos,* v. 6) has the allure of an opening gambit,[28] seemingly functioning in much the same way as "once upon a time" does in much Anglo-Saxon narrative literature.

The prose interlude puts the historical character of John against the broad background of God's creative, revelatory and salvific action. John is introduced as one "sent from God" (John 1:5), and the purpose of his mission is quickly identified: "He came for testimony." The point is immediately reinforced as the author twice employs a purpose clause to state the purpose of John's mission. He is no plenipotentiary envoy. Rather he has been sent by God with a rather specific purpose. John is "to bear witness to the light" (vv. 7, 8).

Those who read the Fourth Gospel in its present format are well aware of this initial characterization of John. They know that John's mission is to be considered within a perspective of cosmic and suprahistorical perspective, but they also know that John's role is that of a witness and only a witness. Their curiosity is whetted when the evangelist solemnly opens the testimony of John with his introductory "And this is the testimony of John." These same

---

[27]See Acts 13:24; 19:4.

[28]In the Greek Bible, the Septuagint (LXX), *egeneto* is the first word of Zechariah, Haggai, Ezekiel, and 1 Maccabees. Preceded by "and" *(kai)*, it is the opening word in Joshua, Judges, 1 Samuel, 2 Samuel, Jonah, Micah, Ruth, and Esther.

readers are also aware of what is really at stake when the evangelist subtly contrasts the figure of John sent by God (1:6) with the priests and Levites sent by Jews from Jerusalem (1:19). The drama is all the more enhanced as the emissaries spar in the Gospel's opening scene. The interrogation is real, but it is, as it were, a confrontation between only the front men.

John's Disciples

The attentive reader of the Fourth Gospel, aware that the evangelist's presentation of the testimony of John is his own formulation and that it differs sharply from the common early Christian description of John, may even entertain the suspicion that the scene so skillfully and so personally painted by the evangelist is a work of his own creation rather than a scene created on the basis of firm historical reminiscence. He or she may be led to wonder whether something in the circumstances attendant upon the composition of the evangelist's work prompted him to cast John in the role of the first Christian witness and uniquely in this role.

Many scholars claim that the makeup of the circles within which the Fourth Gospel was written was hardly homogeneous.[29] Rather, the community of the beloved disciple was a motley group whose membership was constituted by people whose views of Jesus covered a variety of theological hues. To a large extent this membership was ethnically Jewish, but it belonged to a Judaism at various fringes (e.g., the Samaritans). It is not unlikely that this disparate group of Christians with Jewish backgrounds and distinctive theological ideas came into conflict not only with the defenders of Jewish orthodoxy but with other groups as well.

A group of disciples of "John the Baptist" were in existence during the public ministry of Jesus and such groups continued to exist for some time after the foundation of the first Christian Churches.[30] The New Testament attests that John had a follow-

---

[29]See, in this regard, especially the aforementioned works (above, n. 25) of Cullmann and Brown.

[30]See Joseph Thomas, *Le mouvement baptist en Palestine et Syrie (150 av. J.-C.-300 ap. J.-C.)* (Gembloux: Douculot, 1935). In this regard one might also want to cite the role attributed to John the Baptist in the ancient Mandaean literature.

ing and that this following included not only those who came out
on occasion to hear him preach but that it also included some
disciples (Matt 11:2; Luke 7:18-19; John 1:35; 3:25) who were
more or less committed to the movement initiated by John's
preaching. The New Testament accounts, written from a manifestly Christian perspective, show these disciples of John in con-
tact with Jesus. Yet they also clearly attest that not all the disciples
of John became disciples of Jesus. Some inhabitants of the city
of Ephesus in Asia Minor received a Johannine form of baptism,
as distinct from Christian baptism, during the mid-fifties.[31]

John 3:26 indicates that some of the disciples of John were an-
noyed by Jesus' baptizing[32] and the following that Jesus achieved.
Claims as to the messianic status of John seem to have arisen
among some of his disciples.[33] Indeed, the third-century Pseudo-
Clementine *Recognitions* claims that many of the disciples of John
proclaimed him to be the Messiah, and that at least one of them
argued from Jesus' own words (Matt 11:9-11) to prove that John,
and not Jesus, was the Messiah.[34] Although the historicity of all
these traditions merits close scrutiny, it seems quite likely that there
was an ongoing difference of opinion between various Christians
and some of the followers of John the Baptist from fairly early
times. The evangelist's consistent efforts to put John in his place
attest to the tension that existed between the evangelist's own circles and some of John's disciples.[35]

---

[31]Acts 19:1-5; cf. Acts 18:24-25.

[32]John 3:22, 26 are the only indications in the New Testament that Jesus himself actually
baptized. However a corrective note has been added into the Gospel (John 4:2) to the effect
that Jesus' disciples, but not Jesus himself, baptized. This correction and the lack of other
evidence make it likely that the historical Jesus did not in fact baptize, in which case the
controversy to which John 3:25-30 alludes most likely represents a dispute between disciples
of John and members of the Johannine circle.

[33]Cf. Luke 3:15.

[34]*Recognitiones* I, 54, 60 (PG 1, 1238, 1240).

[35]The evangelist also notes that some of John's disciples became disciples of Jesus. See
John 1:37.

John's Place

The evangelist clearly defines John's role when he identifies John as one who is sent to give witness and portrays John "in the docket" acknowledging that his only significant identity is that of the voice. John's testimony to the emissaries of the Pharisees is that he is unworthy to untie the thong of the sandals of the one to come. His words bring to mind the rabbinic maxim that disciples should be willing to perform for their masters any task that a slave would do for his master, except for the menial task of unlacing the sandals.[36] John's testimony bears witness to the tremendous gap in dignity that exists between himself and the one who comes after him.

The contrast between Jesus and John is further highlighted as John, seeing Jesus draw near, enigmatically identifies him as the Lamb of God. Then he goes on to say, "This is he of whom I said, 'After me comes a man who ranks before me, for he was before me' " (John 1:30). With these words John testifies that his own temporal priority vis-à-vis Jesus should not be taken as any indication of his superiority with regard to Jesus. This is, in the evangelist's estimation of things, the repeated testimony of John.[37] The reader of the Gospel in its present format is, of course, aware of the significance of this testimony. Its importance is underscored by its introduction, almost as a note,[38] into the prologue (John 1:15), which John 1:30 repeats in a practically verbatim manner. The note serves to remind the readers of the Gospel that John's testimony is really about the superiority of Jesus.

John 3:25-30

In the presence of his disciples John once again affirms Jesus' superiority when he responds to the concerns that have arisen from

---

[36]Mark 1:7; Luke 3:16; Acts 13:25; cf. Matthew 3:11.

[37]See John 1:30: "this is he of whom *I said* . . . ".

[38]Many such parenthetical remarks occur in the Fourth Gospel. See Gilbert Van Belle, *Les parenthèses dans l'Evangile de Jean: aperçu historique et classification* (Studiorum Novi Testamenti auxilia 11; Louvain: University Press, 1985).

their undue anxiety by saying: "No one can receive anything except what is given him from heaven. You yourselves bear me witness, that I said, I am not the Christ, but I have been sent before him" (John 3:27-28). John's testimony before his own is a reaffirmation of his testimony to the interrogators who had come from the Jews (John 1:20) and the frequently repeated reflection that his mission[39] was that of a precursor.

The scene contains many such flashbacks to the earlier testimony of John. The very locale of John's testimony is recalled.[40] John had given both negative and positive witness to the Christ beyond the Jordan, and both kinds of testimony are recalled in the dialogue between John and his disciples. The net effect is to underscore by repetition the significance of John's testimony. Though repetitive, the scene is hardly redundant. Within the Johannine drama it serves to underscore the notion that John's testimony is intended for his own disciples. Some of them leave to follow Jesus (John 1:37); for those who do not do so, it is necessary for John to repeat his message.

Of the one who is to come after him, though ranking before him, John can only say, "He must increase, but I must decrease" (John 3:30). These words ought to be found on the lips of any Jesus-confessor, but they are particularly significant when found on the lips of John. Many of his disciples claim an exalted status for him, but the evangelist considers John to be the first Jesus-confessor and virtually an honorary member of the Christian circle.[41]

---

[39]Note the use of the verb "send" *(apostellō)* in John 3:28 as in 1:6.

[40]Cf. John 3:26 and 1:28. The consistency with which the evangelist locates the testimony of John "beyond the Jordan" (cf. also John 10:40) is only one aspect of the consistency of characterization to be found in the Fourth Gospel. The constant portrayal of Nicodemus as one who came to Jesus by night is another example of the evangelist's consistency in characterization. See John 3:2; 7:50; 19:39. Cf. R. F. Collins, "The Representative Figures of the Fourth Gospel," *Downside Review* 93 (1976) 26–46, 118–32, p. 37, reprinted in *These Things Have Been Written: Studies in the Fourth Gospel* (Louvain: Theological and Pastoral Monographs, 2; Louvain: Peeters, 16 1990) 1–45, p. 15.

[41]See Ernst Haenchen's commentary apropos John 1:15, where the explanatory note occurs just after the first use of the Johannine "we," i.e., the use of the first person plural to identify the faith conviction of the Johannine circle. Cf. E. Haenchen, *John, 1: A Commentary on the Gospel of John, Chapters 1–6* (Hermeneia; Philadelphia: Fortress, 1984) 116.

One of the striking features of the evangelist's story is the fashion in which he places words on the lips of John. John has testified to the interrogators come from Jerusalem. At the conclusion of each interrogation he has made a forceful statement about himself.[42] Now he testifies for the benefit of his own disciples. They ought to be convinced by the words of their hero himself.

In the evangelist's Gospel story, John's words are particularly significant at this point. The evangelist portrays John as assuaging the fears of his disciples. As he does so, he makes veiled reference to Israel's eschatological expectations. The prophets—especially Hosea, Jeremiah, Isaiah, and Ezekiel[43]—had frequently used the image of marriage in order to describe the unique relationship that existed between Yahweh and his people. The marriage pact was a fitting analogy for the relationship between Yahweh and Israel because the same word, "covenant" *(berith* in Hebrew), was used to describe each of these singular relationships. In each case an elective choice inaugurated the relationship, whose exclusiveness could be highlighted by the recollection of spousal jealousy.[44]

Similar imagery evokes the joyful union of the age to come.[45] The Synoptic tradition uses the imagery of the wedding banquet to denote the messianic era.[46] The Fourth Gospel exploits the traditional marital imagery in its description of the water-made-wine (John 2:1-12),[47] but it is only in John 3:29 that Jesus is specifically represented as the bridegroom.[48] As the friend of the

---

[42]The importance of John's *own* testimony can be especially seen in John 1:23. Whereas Isaiah 40:3 is cited in the Synoptic Gospels as the commentary *about* John, the verse is cited in John 1:23 as a saying *of* John.

[43]Cf. Hosea 1:2-9; 2:4-25; Jeremiah 2:2; 11:15; Isaiah 50:1; 54:5; Ezekiel 16:8-13; Exodus 34:10-16; Deuteronomy 5:2-10.

[44]Deuteronomy 5:9, etc.

[45]Isaiah 62:25; 54:4-6; Hosea 2:3-25; Jeremiah 3:29.

[46]Matthew 22:1-14; 25:1-13; cf. Ephesians 5:25-27.

[47]See Raymond F. Collins, "Cana (Jn. 2:1-12)—The First of His Signs or the Key to His Signs," *Irish Theological Quarterly* 47 (1980) 79-95; *These Things Have Been Written*, 158-82.

[48]In the Cana narrative there is, nonetheless, some slippage in the characterization. Jesus gives way to the bridegroom (vv. 9-10) in such a way that the evangelist intimates that it

bridegroom—the paranymph, whose role was roughly equivalent to that of the best man in our modern weddings—John experiences a full measure of joy. Although full of joy,[49] he is, nonetheless, only the friend of the bridegroom. The bridegroom is the Christ to whom John has borne witness.

John 5:31-36

The evangelist uses yet another rich image to underscore the superiority of Jesus when, in one of his typical monologues, he presents Jesus discoursing at length on the testimony that is borne to him (John 5:31-47). Evoking the interrogation of John instigated by "the Jews,"[50] Jesus speaks about John's testimony: "You sent to John, and he has borne witness to the truth. . . . He was a burning and shining lamp, and you were willing to rejoice for a while in his light" (John 5:33, 35).

John is cited amidst an imposing array of most impressive witnesses to Jesus.[51] He is identified by Jesus himself as one who has borne witness to the truth. There are, however, witnesses even more important than John. One of them consists of the works that the Father has granted Jesus to accomplish. Nonetheless, the witness of John is very important. John can be compared to "a burning and shining lamp." Although some have reveled in his light, he is not the light itself,[52] he is only a lamp. As John him-

---

is Jesus himself who is the bridegroom. Cf. R. F. Collins, "Cana" p. 90 *(These Things Have Been Written,* 178), and P. Geoltrain, " 'Les noces à Cana. Jean 2,1-12.' Analyse des structures narratives," *Foi et vie* 73 (1974) 83-90.

[49]In the biblical tradition, joy is a characteristic attitude of those who stand in the salvific presence of God.

[50]The "you" to whom the present monologue is addressed are "the Jews" (cf. John 5:10; 17); it is they who sent a delegation to John (John 5:33a and 1:19).

[51]Five different witnesses to Jesus are cited in the review. Altogether there are some seven witnesses to Jesus cited in the Fourth Gospel, that is, John, the Father, Jesus, his works, the Scriptures, the Spirit, and the disciples, including the evangelist. Some see this selection as an indication of the evangelist's preferential use of the number seven as a principle of organization. See F.-M. Braun, *Jean le théologien,* 2 (Etudes bibliques; Paris: Gabalda, 1964) 13-15. See also Urban C. von Wahlde, "The Witnesses to Jesus in John 5:31-40 and Belief in the Fourth Gospel," *Catholic Biblical Quarterly* 43 (1981) 385-404.

[52]See John 1:8: "He was not the light, but came to bear witness to the light."

self has testified that he is only the friend of the bridegroom, not the bridegroom, so now Jesus equivalently affirms that John is not the light, he is only the lamp.

John 10:40-42

Finally, in a restful interlude in the drama which the evangelist has been unfolding before his readers' eyes and which is about to move quickly toward its climax as he tells the story of Lazarus who was raised from the dead (John 11:1–12:11), the evangelist recalls that Jesus again went away into the region beyond the Jordan (John 10:40-42). This is the area in which John had been baptizing.[53] As such, it is a fitting locale for yet another comparison between John and Jesus. This time, it is "the many" *(polloi)* who make the point. The many are those who believe in Jesus.[54] They acknowledge, as did Jesus (John 5:33), that the testimony of John is true. Nonetheless, this authentic witness to Jesus pales in comparison to the one to whom John has borne witness. Jesus performs many signs,[55] but "John did no sign" (John 10:41). He is clearly in a different category from Jesus.

The evangelist has, therefore, effectively put John in his place. That place is that of the witness par excellence, and John fulfills this role in fulfillment of a divine mandate. It is a role John publicly accepts, even in an openly hostile forum. That John is a witness, and only a witness, entails a great gap between himself and Jesus, to whom he bears witness. The difference between the two is acknowledged by Jesus and the many and is formally attested by John, who tells his own disciples, "He must increase, but I must decrease."

The evangelist thus cleverly portrays John as personally proclaiming both his own role as witness and the otherness of the

---

[53]See John 1:28 and 3:26. The Synoptic narratives are totally silent about any trips of Jesus beyond the Jordan. See, however, Matthew 19:1; Mark 10:1.

[54]See John 2:23; 4:39; 6:60, 66; 7:31; 8:30; 10:42; 12:11, 42.

[55]That Jesus performed different signs is an important motif in the evangelist's narrative. He has chosen and highlighted seven such signs: the water made wine in Cana, the cure of the royal official's son, the cure of the man born blind, the multiplication of loaves, the walking on water, the cure of the lame man, and the raising of Lazarus.

one to whom he bears witness. John personally acknowledges this role before a hostile audience (John 1:19-28), in a somewhat neutral setting (John 1:29-34), and, repeatedly, before his own disciples (John 1:35-36; 3:25-30). In every instance, John has the emphatic "last word" (John 1:23, 27-28, 34; 3:29). His words testify to Jesus as the coming one and the Son of God. As John fulfills this role, he becomes the first Christian witness.

John's Testimony About Jesus

Having opened his narrative with the scenario of a double interrogation by the Jews with the double confession by John, the evangelist moves his account rapidly forward as he describes a chain of events that lead up to a dramatic statement by Jesus himself: "Truly, truly, I say to you, you will see heaven opened, and the angels of God ascending and descending upon the Son of Man" (John 1:51).

The movement toward this climax is staged within the temporal setting of a week, as the evangelist moves his readers from one day to the next (John 1:29, 35, 43). Events follow one another rapidly as John gives his positive testimony about Jesus (1:29-34), two of his disciples follow Jesus (1:35-39), one of them seeks out his brother and brings him to Jesus (1:40-42), Jesus calls Philip (1:43-44), and Philip seeks out Nathanael (1:45-50). The consequence of John's testimony is a series of encounters with Jesus, which the evangelist describes artfully and dramatically. The continuity in the chain reaction is highlighted as only one of the characters in any encounter leaves the scene; the other remains behind to form a literary and dramatic link with the preceding scene.

What is the testimony that unleashes this series of events? It is "Behold, the Lamb of God" (John 1:29, 36). The saying is enigmatic and scholars cannot agree on the meaning of the metaphor. Some think of the apocalyptic lamb that serves as a motif in some apocalyptic literature.[56] Others think of the lamb that was sacrificed daily in the Temple. Still others think that "the Lamb"

---

[56] See *T. Jos.* 19:8; Revelation 5:6.

represents a mistranslation of "servant" at some indeterminate point in the oral tradition behind the Fourth Gospel.[57] Finally, there are those who think that the evangelist is making reference to the paschal Lamb, to which allusion is made in John 19:36. While there is relatively little possibility of secure exit from the impasse over the correct interpretation of John's "Lamb of God,"[58] there can be little doubt that the evangelist has characterized John as a prophet and a seer, making use of a revelation formula with five characteristic elements: " . . . saw . . . [someone] coming . . . said . . . 'Behold . . . [symbol].' "[59] The use of this revelation formula with its enigmatic identification of Jesus as "the Lamb of God" effectively casts John in the role of a prophet and represents a radically different casting of John's prophetic role from that found in the Synoptics, where the prophet John announces the coming of the kingdom and calls people to repentance.[60]

As a prophet, John must interpret the symbol he has used, much as the prophets of old had made use of enigmatic symbols,[61] which they then had to interpret for the people. When the evangelist portrays John in the role of interpreting the symbol he has employed, he shows John recalling both his previous testimony and his previous visionary experience: "This is he of whom I said, 'After me comes a man who ranks before me, for he was before me.' . . . And I have seen and have borne witness that this is

---

[57]The Aramaic word *talyâ* can mean either "servant" or "lamb." If the mistranslation hypothesis is accepted, the engimatic saying would recall the Deutero-Isaian Servant of Yahweh, to which allusion is made in the Synoptic's description of Jesus' baptism.

[58]I am inclined to favor, slightly, the view that the paschal lamb is the principal referent of the metaphor. John's words "who takes away the sin of the world" apparently make reference to the passion of Jesus. Indeed, the evangelist's entire narrative is pervaded by the thought of Jesus' passion-glorification. (See R. F. Collins, "John's Gospel: A Passion Narrative?" *The Bible Today* 24 (1986) 181–86; *These Things Have Been Written*, 87–93. The Johannine passion narrative, however, includes a clear reference to the paschal lamb, namely in the patently Johannine reference to Exodus 12:10, 46 (see Ps 34:21) in John 19:36.

[59]See John 1:29, 36, 47; 19:26-27 (cf. Michel de Goedt, "Un schème de révélation dans le quatrième évangile," *New Testament Studies* 8 (1961–62) 142–50.

[60]Matthew 3:2-4; 11:9-10; 21:26; Mark 1:2-4 (cf. v. 6); 12:32; Luke 1:76; 3:2-6 (cf. v. 8); 7:26-27; 20:6; Acts 13:24.

[61]Isaiah 8:18; 20:3; Jeremiah 13:1-11; Ezekiel 4:1-4; 12:1-16; 24:15-17; 37:15-22.

the Son of God" (John 1:30, 34). The one who gives testimony is an eyewitness (see John 1:32, 43).[62]

The evangelist's narrative emphasis lies on John. Repeatedly his Greek-language text employs words and particles whose function is emphatic.[63] The evangelist wants to highlight the place of John in the divine scheme and carefully suggests that John has fulfilled a prophetic role. In the evangelist's view of things, that prophetic role is in function of John's role as a witness.

The identity of the one whom John, the prophetic witness, so mysteriously qualifies as the Lamb of God is one whom he has not recognized, and whom he would not have recognized were it not for the vision and the key to the vision provided by God. Behind this scene apparently stands a Jewish tradition about the hidden Messiah.[64] Even if the Messiah were to be present, he would remain unknown until the time of his manifestation.[65] John's apparent role is to make the Messiah known (John 1:31); it is for that he has been sent (John 1:6).

Since the Messiah remains hidden, even from the one sent to bear witness to him—at the beginning of the evangelist's narrative the Messiah's identity seems also to be unknown to the official interrogators[66]—it is fitting that the God who has sent John to bear witness identify the one to whom he is to give testimony. That the word of God comes to John further characterizes him as a prophet.[67] The sign of identification is to be the descent of the Spirit, and John is to be the beneficiary of the vision of the descending Spirit: "He on whom you see the Spirit descend and remain, this is he who baptizes with the Holy Spirit" (John 1:33).

John is gifted with this experience and subsequently bears witness to the event that enables him to fulfill his divinely appointed function of bearing witness to the Messiah. Having heard the word

---

[62]Cf. John 19:35.

[63]*Egō* (v. 30). *kagō* (vv. 31, 33, 34).

[64]See John 1:31, 33.

[65]See various passages in Jewish apocalyptic literature (e.g. *Pss. Sol.* 18:5) and Justin's *Dialogue with Trypho,* VIII, 4 (PG 6, 729-30). Cf. John 7:27.

[66]See John 1:19-25.

[67]Cf. Jeremiah 1:4; Ezekiel 1:3; etc.

of God, the prophet can speak of his unique experience and of its real meaning: "I saw the Spirit descend as a dove from heaven, and it remained on him. . . . And I have seen and have borne witness that this is the Son of God" (John 1:32, 34). The title "Son of God" bears witness to the unique relationship that exists between Jesus and God, identifying Jesus as one with and through whom God works in a particularly significant fashion.

Characterization

The evangelist has offered his readers a crafted description of the role of John as prophet. Since the evangelist reserves to Jesus the title of prophet (John 1:21, 25; 4:19, 44; 6:14; 7:40 (cf. verse 52); 9:17),[68] he consistently refuses to call John a prophet (John 1:21). Nevertheless, the evangelist clearly intimates that John is indeed a prophetic figure. John is someone to whom the word of God has come, someone who speaks the word of the Lord, who utters revelatory statements, and who interprets enigmatic symbols. While suggesting that John is a prophet, the evangelist nonetheless fully subordinates John's prophetic status to his role as a witness.

In similar fashion, the evangelist makes no mention whatsoever of the tradition that John baptized Jesus. Indeed, the entire Gospel does not offer any clue that Jesus was baptized,[69] let alone that he was baptized by John. In the evangelist's eyes, John's role is to bear witness to Jesus, not to baptize him.

There are, nonetheless, certain similarities between the fourth evangelist's tale of the encounter between John and Jesus and the Synoptists' description of Jesus' baptism. One of the most striking is undoubtedly the importance of the descent of the Spirit in

---

[68]The description of Jesus as the prophet undoubtedly responds to the expectations of the Samaritan components within the Johannine circle. Cf. Marie-Emile Boismard, *Moïse ou Jésus: Essai de christologie johannique* (Bibliotheca Ephemeridum Theologicarum Lovaniensium 84; Louvain: University Press, 1988) 7–11.

[69]The tradition is nonetheless well attested in the New Testament. See Matthew 3:13-17; Mark 1:9-11; Luke 3:21-22; Acts 1:22. The Lukan tradition does not specifically identify John as the one who baptized Jesus. Nonetheless, Jesus' baptism by John is a historical fact whose historicity is confirmed by the apologetic dialogue that Matthew introduces in Matthew 3:14-15.

all four accounts. According to the fourth evangelist, the descent and abiding presence of the Spirit upon Jesus constitutes the sign by which Jesus is recognized as the Son to God. Nevertheless, the fourth evangelist's account differs from those of the other evangelists in two major respects. First, only the fourth evangelist portrays John as the privileged visionary of the descent of the Spirit.[70] Secondly, the evangelist underscores the fact that the Spirit not only descends on Jesus, it also remains on him. The abiding presence of the Spirit distinguishes Jesus[71] from other prophetic figures to whom the Spirit is given for a time. This abiding presence of the Spirit upon Jesus is John's experience, and it is an indicated part of the identifying sign.

If the evangelist has omitted any specific reference to the baptism of Jesus,[72] the omission is probably due to the polemics between the members of his Christian community and the disciples of John who refused to recognize Jesus as the Christ. The fact that the evangelist places John's visionary experience[73] at some point in time prior to the encounter described in John 1:29-34 also serves to distance John's testimony from the baptism of Jesus, an event whose occurrence, surely known to the members of the evangelist's own community, was undoubtedly well emphasized by the fervent disciples of John.

Prior to the encounter portrayed in John 1:29-34,[74] John has already testified to the coming one (John 1:30)[75] and has identi-

---

[70]In Matthew (3:16) and Mark (1:10) it is Jesus himself who sees the Spirit descend. In Luke the descent of the Spirit is described in such a way that all the people (among whom John is presumably not to be counted, cf. Luke 3:20) could see it.

[71]Cf. Isaiah 11:2; *1 Enoch* 49:3; *T. Levi* 18:7.

[72]Since the Johannine tradition seems to have been at least generally familiar with the Synoptic tradition, it is quite likely that the evangelist deliberately chose to omit any reference to Jesus' baptism.

[73]Note the perfect tense of the verbs in vv. 32 and 34, "I saw" *(tetheamai)* and "I have seen" *(heóraka)*.

[74]Note the use of the aorist tense of the verb in v. 30, "I said" *(eipon)* and the perfect tense of the verb in v. 34, "I have testified" *(memartureka)*. Normally the perfect tense indicates a past action which has enduring effects.

[75]The identification of Jesus as "the coming one" *(ho erchomenos)* is an important theme in the Fourth Gospel. See John 1:15, 27; 3:31 (twice); 6:6, 35, 37; 11:27; 12:13.

fied the one to come as the Son of God (John 1:34). In synthetic fashion, the encounter highlights the significance of John's positive testimony to Jesus. It is Jesus who comes to John. John testifies to who and what Jesus really is.

The evangelist is quite consistent[76] in his portrayal of John. He has reduced his role to that of a witness who has no real mission other than to bear testimony to Jesus. He bears his testimony, in positive and negative fashion, to those who are hostile and to those who follow him with devotion, and he testifies repeatedly to the same realities. He has been put in his place by the evangelist. That place is at once an exalted place and a limited place— exalted because John has been sent by God to bear witness, limited because he has been sent *only* to bear witness. He is the prototypical witness, but he is only a witness. In the evangelist's view of things, John is not really John the Baptist, he is John the witness.

---

[76]According to Aristotle, consistency is one of the qualities an author should seek to achieve in the portrayal of a character. Cf. *Poetics,* 1454a.

2

The First Disciples

After his exposé of the nature of John's witness, the evangelist turns his attention—and the reader's—to a reflection on the results of John's testimony. The first scene he narrates is innocent enough on the surface. It tells the story of two of John's disciples who are so impressed by John's testimony that they follow after Jesus. In his rendition of the scene the evangelist leaves both disciples nameless, thereby accentuating the apparent innocence of his narrative.

The Story

Underlying the evangelist's story there probably lies the memory of some of John's disciples who had affiliated themselves with the Jesus movement. Nonetheless, the scene as the evangelist describes it conjures up more than merely a vague reminiscence of the past. The story is paradigmatic in that the evangelist shares with his readers his vision of discipleship. The dramatic character of his narrative increases as he makes use of the chosen setting of a week. Events happen rapidly one after another as the evangelist sets out in sequence the story of the first disciples, the call of Peter, the call of Philip, and the call of Nathanael, after which the entire chapter concludes with a majestic statement of Jesus' self-revelation: "Truly, truly, I say to you, you will see heaven opened, and the angels of God ascending and descending upon the Son of man" (John 1:51).

Long before the crescendo reaches this climax, the evangelist picks up on John's testimony. The scene portrayed in verse 36, "He looked at Jesus as he walked, and said, 'Behold the Lamb of God!'" is a virtual repeat of the scene described in verse 29—except that it takes place on the next day. The repeated staging, within a different temporal setting, is an integral part of what is sometimes called the evangelist's "circular style." He constantly returns to the same themes, looking at them from different perspectives as he explores and attempts to share with his readers the manifold richness of the realities about which he is writing.

A classic example of the evangelist's use of a repeated scene temporally situated on different days is his account of the Risen Jesus' appearances to his disciples. A first scene describes the disciples shut up in a room when Jesus appears to them (John 20:19). Subsequently, the evangelist develops his narrative in such a way as to show that Jesus' resurrection results in the mission of his disciples and the gift of the Spirit to them (John 20:20-23). Shortly thereafter[1] the evangelist tells his readers that "eight days later, his disciples were again in the house, and . . . the doors were shut, but Jesus came and stood among them, and said, 'Peace be with you'" (John 20:26). This is a virtual repeat of the scene described in verse 19, but now the evangelist contemplates the doubt of the disciples,[2] represented in the Fourth Gospel by the doubting Thomas.[3]

John 1:35-36 has a function similar to that of John 20:26. In both instances, after an indication of time (the next day, eight days later), there is to be found the telltale adverb "again" *(palin)*. Then comes the repetition of the setting presented a few verses earlier (1:29; 20:19) along with the introduction of new personalities (the two disciples, Thomas). The appearance of these newly introduced characters allows the evangelist to develop his theme

---

[1]John 20:24-25 obviously represents a transition from one scene to the other. As an element of Johannine style, it functions in much the same way as "Now that days was the sabbath" does in John 5:9. This short sentence is appended to the previous narrative (John 5:1-9a), virtually complete in itself, as an introduction to the extended discourse to follow.

[2]See Matthew 28:17; Mark 16:11, 14; Luke 24:36-43.

[3]See R. F. Collins, "The Representative Figures of the Fourth Gospel," *Downside Review* 93 (1976) 124-26; *These Things Have Been Written*, 35-38.

in a new manner. As he first develops the significance of Jesus' resurrection for the mission of his disciples and then turns to the theme of the disciples' doubt, so now, after having developed the significance of John's testimony, he turns to the result of that testimony. The effect of his testimony upon the two disciples of verse 35 encapsulates the evangelist's vision of what the effect of John's testimony ought to be.

On the narrative level[4] the story is remarkably easy to comprehend. John, whose teaching has apparently attracted several disciples[5] as well as the interest of the authorities in Jerusalem, is standing about with two of his disciples. The evangelist has not specifically located the scene he is about to describe, but it is most likely in Bethany beyond the Jordan, the typical locale of John's activity. Moreover, the evangelist has not indicated any shift in the setting of his scenes thus far. The evangelist's silence in this regard is significant. He usually describes the movement of his characters.[6] Such movement not only contributes to his story line but also serves to increase the drama of the tale he is unfolding.

John, upon whom the evangelist's story has focused since he began his Gospel in earnest at 1:19,[7] is described as "standing" *(heistēkei)*. It is almost as if he is waiting for something to happen.[8] This impression is all the more likely insofar as the evangelist does not immediately describe any interaction[9] between John and the two disciples. In fact, the relative immobility of the three characters contrasts sharply with the action soon to follow: "Jesus walked . . . they followed. . . . Jesus turned . . . them following, . . . 'Come and see.' . . . They came and saw."

---

[4]See R. F. Collins, "Discipleship in John's Gospel," *Emmanuel* 91 (1985) 248-55; in *These Things Have Been Written,* 46-55.

[5]A disciple *(mathētēs)* is, literally, one who learns, a pupil.

[6]Cf. John 1:43; 2:12; 2:23; etc.

[7]The prologue is an obvious addition to the Gospel, see R. F. Collins, "The Oldest Commentary on the Fourth Gospel," *The Bible Today* 98 (1978) 1769-75; in *These Things Have Been Written,* 151-57.

[8]Cf. John 18:16; 20:11.

[9]The reader of the Gospel will certainly note that the only significant action undertaken by John is that of giving witness. In the present scene that action does not take place until Jesus makes his appearance.

As the scene opens, all the attention is riveted on John. He has been the main character thus far, the thread that ties the various scenes together. Now, by means of a verb in the singular[10] the evangelist once again throws the spotlight on John. As on the previous day, John sees Jesus walking. Once again John proclaims Jesus to be the Lamb of God. Whereas the previous scene had spelled out the significance of this enigmatic utterance, the present scene unfolds the consequences of John's announcement.

The two disciples—in fact, all of the disciples on scene at the moment—hear John's pronouncement and follow after Jesus. Although they have not previously appeared in the narrative, the evangelist would apparently have his readers understand that these two nameless disciples have heard John's repeated testimony about the one to come and have identified Jesus as the coming one because of John's mysterious demonstrative utterance.

Aware of the difference between the mere voice and the one about whom the voice had testified, the two disciples follow after Jesus. At this point, the reader's attention, hitherto focused on John and his disciples, now focuses on Jesus and those same disciples. The evangelist's adherence to the law of stage duality has facilitated this dramatic shift of focus. As of verse 37b, the reader's interest is fully focused on the interaction between Jesus and those who had been John's disciples.

Having left John, the pair follow after Jesus. Apparently hearing the footfalls, Jesus turns to see them following. He makes the obvious inquiry, "What are you looking for?"[11] The pursuers call him "Rabbi" and ask where he is staying. Rather than give a straightforward answer, Jesus invites his pursuers to come and see where he is staying. As the evangelist narrates the story, the pair take Jesus up on his invitation and accompany him to the still-unnamed place where he is staying. It is already late in the

---

[10]The focus on John is even more accentuated in the Greek text than it is in the English translation. Not only has the evangelist used a verb in the singular *(heistēkei)*, but he has once again cited the name of John. Since the form of the Greek verb already includes a third-person-singular subject, the introduction of the name serves to emphasize that it was John who was standing.

[11]So *ti zēteite* is translated in the NEB. It is aptly rendered as "what do you want?" in the JB, NJB, and NIV.

afternoon by the time they arrive,[12] so they stay until sundown and presumably spend the night.

Jesus the Rabbi

The short dialogue is intriguing. Dialogue with questions and even repeated questions is a feature of the evangelist's style. One striking element in this dialogue between Jesus and John's former disciples is that they call Jesus "Rabbi." "Sir" *(kurie)* is the term commonly used in respectful direct address, and the evangelist often adopts this expression of conventional politeness in his descriptions of Jesus' "chance" encounters. Even those who benefit from Jesus' superhuman power address Jesus as "Sir."[13] Now, however, the pursuers respond to Jesus' question by calling him "Rabbi." The formal address means "teacher" *(didaskalos)*. As is his custom, the evangelist translates the transliterated Hebrew term for the benefit of his readers.[14] The Hebrew term literally means "my master" and was often used of an esteemed teacher by his students. Later, of course, the term came simply to mean "teacher," and it is commonly used in this sense today.

Nothing thus far in the Gospel narrative has indicated that Jesus, metaphorically described as the Lamb of God, was a teacher. Nothing suggests that the people expected the coming one to be a teacher. There was much speculation in the air about the coming Messiah, but the book on him was that he was to be a political or military leader. Nevertheless, as the evangelist now describes his scene, the disciples of John address Jesus as "Rabbi," "my teacher."

In the Fourth Gospel the term is used rather infrequently. Seven of its eight occurrences are to be found on the lips of Jesus' dis-

---

[12]By ordinary computations, the 10th hour would be about 4 P.M. Given the Jewish manner of reckoning time, however, the 12 hours of the day represent, not exactly 720 minutes, but the entire period between sunrise and sunset. Thus the 10th hour means that five-sixths of the daylight period has already passed.

[13]See John 4:11, 15, 19, 49; 5:7; 6:34; (8:11); 9:36, 38; 20:15. Philip is likewise addressed as "Sir" in John 12:21. There are, however, passages in the Fourth Gospel where *Kurie* is more accurately rendered "Lord," since it implies an acceptance of Jesus in faith. Cf. John 6:68; 11:3, 12, 21, 27, 32, 34, 39; 13:6, 9, 25, 36, 37; 14:5, 8, 22; 21:15, 16, 17, 20, 21.

[14]See John 1:38, 41, 42; 4:25; 5:2; 9:7; 11:16; 19:13, 17; 20:16, 24; 21:2. Cf. 19:20.

ciples.[15] The other is placed on the lips of those disciples who acknowledge John as their teacher (John 3:26). When, therefore, the pursuers call upon Jesus as "Rabbi," the evangelist seems to intimate that they have switched allegiance. They are no longer disciples of John; they have become disciples of Jesus.

A pair of disciples

That the nameless pair have indeed become disciples of Jesus is further intimated by the evangelist, who writes of them as having "followed" Jesus. In common Greek parlance, "to follow"*(akoloutheō)* meant to go after someone or, when used of things, to follow from or be consequent upon. Occasionally, for example in Thucydides and some other ancient authors, the verb is used in a metaphorical sense. The metaphorical use predominates in the New Testament: To be a follower of Jesus is to be a disciple of Jesus. Nonetheless, the use of the verb "to follow" in the description of Jesus' disciples was particularly adequate to their real situation during the ministry of Jesus. Jesus' followers literally "followed after" the itinerant preacher.

The use of the verb "to follow" as a characteristic description of discipleship is perhaps best encapsulated in the authoritative command "follow me." That is the call to discipleship, addressed to the grieving son (Matt 8:22; Luke 9:59), the tax collector (Matt 9:9; Mark 2:14; Luke 5:27), and the rich young man (Matt 19:21; Mark 10:21; Luke 18:22). In the Fourth Gospel, this call is addressed to Philip (John 1:43) and Peter (John 21:19, 22).

This distinctive language is part of the technical vocabulary of the early Church;[16] hence, the fourth evangelist is respecting early Christian usage when he describes Jesus' disciples as those who

[15]John 1:38, 49; 3:2; 4:31; 6:25; 9:2; 11:8. Among these, John 3:2 is a special case, since Nicodemus ultimately proves to be a nonbeliever or, at best, a cryptic believer (see Collins, "Representative Figures," 36–37 [*These Things Have Been Written,* 14–16] and "Jesus' Conversation with Nicodemus," *The Bible Today* 93 [1977] 149–67; in *These Things Have Been Written,* 56–67).

[16]Mark, followed by Matthew, uses another expression to describe the call of Peter and Andrew. In that case (Matt 4:19; Mark 1:17), the "follow me" of most English translations represents the Greek *deute opisō mou,* literally, "come after me." The two expressions are virtually interchangeable. Cf. Mark 8:34 and parallels.

follow after him. Generally—that is, apart from two merely narrative uses[17]—the evangelist uses the verb "to follow" *(akoloutheō)* in such a way as to connote discipleship.[18] Thus, it is particularly significant that the evangelist portrays the disciples of John as having left John in order to follow after Jesus.

Instead of following John, these disciples now follow Jesus. They had learned from John; now they are to learn from Jesus. Hence, they can call him "Rabbi." This shift in allegiance indicates that in the eyes of the fourth evangelist, following Jesus implies just as much radical commitment as it does for the Synoptic authors. The Synoptists describe Jesus challenging his would-be disciples to abandon all their worldly possessions as an enabling condition for real discipleship (Matt 19:21; Mark 10:21; Luke 18:22). They show a Jesus who asks that his disciples even forgo the child's responsibility to bury a dead parent (Matt 8:22; Luke 9:60). They describe Jesus' disciples as having abandoned their nets[19] or their taxcollector's table.[20] In similar fashion, the fourth evangelist portrays Jesus' disciples as having abandoned their allegiance to John.

The Synoptic stories of the call of the first disciples are undoubtedly syncopated narratives, so told as to emphasize that radical decision is an important quality of true discipleship.[21] In much the same way, the fourth evangelist highlights the radicality of discipleship as he tells the story of John's former disciples. One is a disciple of Jesus *or* one is a disciple of John. There is no compromise. A disciple of Jesus cannot have it both ways.

Yet there is more to the evangelist's story than merely the expression of his vision that radical commitment is a quality of discipleship. In his tale of the two disciples who leave John to follow after Jesus, the evangelist expresses his conviction that those who

---

[17]John 11:31; 20:6.

[18]John 1:37, 38, 40, 43; 6:2; 8:12; 10:4, 5, 27; 12:26; 13:36 (twice), 37; 18:15; 21:20; however, further precision has to be brought to bear in the case of 6:2; 18:15; and 21:20.

[19]Matthew 4:18-22; Mark 1:16-20; Luke 5:11.

[20]Matthew 9:9-13; Mark 2:13-17; Luke 5:27-32.

[21]See also Matthew 8:21-22 (parallel, Luke 9:59-62) and Matthew 19:21 (parallels, Mark 10:21; Luke 18:22).

have truly learned from John, those who have really understood the meaning of John's testimony, become disciples of Jesus. John's disciples find their real place in life as disciples of Jesus.[22]

The realization that there is a level of meaning in the narrative beyond that of the story line might prompt the discerning reader of the Fourth Gospel to ask whether the evangelist has more to say than immediately meets the eye. Does he have a hidden agenda? The answer is yes. In this case, it is to affirm that those who have been truly attentive to the Johannine witness ought to join the circle of Jesus' disciples.

In addition to this hidden agenda, it is apparent that the evangelist uses symbolic language, as when the testimony of John is given symbolic expression in the verbal symbol "Lamb of God." Nonetheless, the evangelist's use of symbolic language seems to be more pervasive than the merely occasional use of such blatant symbols as the enigmatic "Lamb of God."

Symbolism

Many commentators have written about the symbolism of the Fourth Gospel. They often draw attention to the number of verbal expressions in the Fourth Gospel that have both a narrative and a symbolic sense.[23] A classic example is the evangelist's use of the verb "to lift up" *(hupsō;* John 3:14 (twice); 8:28; 12:32, 34), which means simultaneously "to lift up on the cross" and "to be raised unto glory." The use of double entendres is part of the fabric of the Fourth Gospel. This choice of symbolic language allows the evangelist to impart a theological depth of meaning to a story that makes eminent sense on the narrative level.

---

[22]A point otherwise made with respect to those who faithfully awaited the coming of the messianic era in the symbolic narrative at the foot of the cross. See John 19:26-27 and Collins, "Representative Figures," 121-22; *These Things Have Been Writte,* 31-33.

[23]Cf. David W. Wead, *The Literary Devices in John's Gospel* (Theologische Dissertationen, 4; Basel: Reinhardt, 1970) 30-70; Sandra M. Schneiders, "History and Symbolism in the Fourth Gospel," in M. de Jonge, ed., *L'Evangile de Jean: Sources, rédaction, théologie* (Bibliotheca Ephemeridum Theologicarum Lovaniensium, 44; Louvain: University Press, 1977) 371-76; R. F. Collins, "The Search for Jesus: Reflections on the Fourth Gospel," *Laval théologique et philosophique* 34 (1978) 27-48, esp. 29-30; in *These Things Have Been Written,* 94-127, esp. 96-99.

Thus it is appropriate to think of two levels in the Fourth Gospel, the narrative and the symbolic. Given the evangelist's predilection for symbols and for words with a double meaning, it is often the case that the truly literal meaning of a narrative in the Fourth Gospel is in its symbolic sense.

The scenario presented by the evangelist in John 1:35-39 is one whose vocabulary is, to a very large extent, composed of words with a double meaning. In addition to *"follow"(akoloutheō)*, *"seek" (zēteō)*, *"stay" (menō)*, and *"see" (horaō)* are verbs with a double meaning.[24] The abundance of such symbolic vocabulary makes the reader realize that as the evangelist narrates his tale of Jesus' first disciples,[25] he intends to share more than a merely factual description of an encounter that took place long before his Gospel was set in writing.

The Search for Jesus

Jesus' initial question is intriguing. He ask his pursuers "What do you seek?"—a question that on the merely narrative level means "what you want?" or "what are you looking for?" No real answer is given, because the pursuers respond with a question, "Where are you staying?" Jesus' opening gambit becomes even more intriguing when the Fourth Gospel is compared with the Synoptics. In each of these Gospels the first public utterance of Jesus (Matt 3:15; Mark 1:15; Luke 4:21) is programmatic for the entire Gospel story.[26] Might not this be the situation in the Fourth Gospel as well? That this might indeed be the case is suggested quite strongly by some ancient Greek manuscripts,[27] which offer "whom do you seek?" as Jesus' first question.

---

[24] See Collins, "Discipleship."

[25] The Fourth Gospel's story of these first disciples is quite different from that found in the Synoptic Gospels, where Jesus is presented as first calling two pairs of fishermen (Matt 4:18-22; Mark 1:16-20). Even that story lends itself to a symbolic interpretation. Luke seems to have done so by interweaving with it the story of a miraculous catch of fish (Luke 5:1-11). Common to the stories of Matthew, Mark, and John is the figure of Andrew (Matt 4:18; Mark 1:16; John 1:40). Andrew is, however, absent from the Lukan tale.

[26] See Collins, "The Search," 27–28; *These Things Have Been Written*, 94–96.

[27] Especially the ninth-century Codex Koridethi. Cf. John 18:4, 7; 20:15.

"To seek" *(zeteō)* is a word often found in the Fourth Gospel, where it occurs thirty-four times.[28] It is one of the evangelist's characteristic expressions, usually found in passages clearly composed by the evangelist or in passages that, if not of his firsthand composition, at least bear marked evidence of his editorial work.

"To seek" *(zeteō)* is commonly used in Greek for the ordinary looking for things that are lost or misplaced, but the verb was also used to describe philosophical study and the religious quest. Philo of Alexandria, the first-century Alexandrian Jew, used the verb to bring together the Hellenistic philosopher's intellectual quest and the Hebrew's heart seeking for God. In the Greek Bible (LXX), "to seek" became almost a technical term for the search for God, especially in the Wisdom literature where the search for Divine Wisdom is a striking motif.[29]

"To seek" is also a translation of the Hebrew verb *darash,* a word found in the phrase *darash ha Torah* of Jewish literature. The phrase is often found in the Dead Sea Scrolls,[30] where it has become a technical term for the study and interpretation of the Scriptures. "To seek the Torah" is to interpret the Scriptures.

In light of the way the verb "to seek" was used, it is quite plausible that the evangelist is portraying John's former disciples as individuals who are in pursuit of Divine Wisdom. For the evangelist, however, it is Jesus who embodies Divine Wisdom.[31] Ironically (since the readers of the Gospel are presumably well aware that Jesus embodies Divine Wisdom) those seekers of Divine Wisdom find Wisdom personified when they go in pursuit of Jesus.

Yet the evangelist also presents Jesus as an interpreter of the Scriptures,[32] principally in reference to himself. The Jesus of the

---

[28] John 1:39; 4:23, 27; 5:18, 30, 44; 6:24, 26; 7:1, 4, 11, 18 (twice), 19, 20, 25, 30, 34, 36; 8:21, 37, 40, 50 (twice); 10:39; 11:8, 56, 13:33; 16:19; 18:4, 7, 8; 19:12; 20:15.

[29] See Wisdom 1:1-2a; 8:2, 18; etc.

[30] 1QS 6:6; 4QFl 1:11; CD 6:7; 7:118. Cf. 1QS 5:11; 6:7; 8:24; 1QH 2:15, 32; 4QpNah 2:7; CD 1:18.

[31] See Collins, "The Search," 35–36; *These Things Have Been Written,* 106–09.

[32] Cf. Peder Borgen, *Bread from Heaven: An Exegetical Study of the Concept of Manna in the Gospel of John and the Writings of Philo* (Supplements to Novum Testamentum, 10; Leiden: Brill, 1965); Bruce J. Malina, *The Palestinian Manna Tradition: The Manna Tradition in the Palestinian Targums and Its Relationship to the New Testament Writings* (Leiden: Brill, 1968).

Fourth Gospel, for example, offers an extended Midrash on Psalm 78:24 in the bread of life discourse (John 6:26-51). From this perspective—that is, from the global understanding of Jesus shared by the evangelist and his community—it is not unlikely that the pair of disciples are portrayed as going to Jesus as one who can interpret the Scriptures. If so, they would most likely address him as "Rabbi," the very title found in the address of John 1:38. The use of this title certainly reflects the understanding of Jesus entertained by the members of the evangelist's community.

Jesus' Abode

To Jesus' question "What do you seek?," the disciples answer, "Where are you staying?"[33] Their interrogative response is not as innocuous as it may seem on first reading. "To stay"*(menō)* is a word the evangelist often uses. It appears to be a term that enjoyed particular currency in his circles, since it occurs sixty-seven times in the Johannine writings, including forty times in the Fourth Gospel,[34] but it is to be found only fifty-one times in the rest of the New Testament.

Although the evangelist occasionally uses the term in the ordinary sense of "to stay" or "to live," he most often uses it in such a way that it bears profound theological meaning. For the evangelist, "to stay" *(menō)*[35] normally suggests a particularly important moment in the history of salvation. Jesus stays with disciples who believe in him (John 2:12; 4:40; 7:9; 10:40; 11:6, 54; 14:25).

Many who have translated the Fourth Gospel into English have attempted to capture something of the rich theological sense of the evangelist's language by using the word "abide" to translate the Greek verb. The crowds proclaim that the Christ abides forever (John 12:34), but the evangelist suggests that Jesus abides

---

[33]JB and NJB translate the question "where do you live?"

[34]John 1:32, 33, 38, 39 (twice); 2:12; 3:36; 4:40 (twice); 5:38; 6:27, 56; 7:9; 8:31, 35 (twice); 9:41; 10:40; 11:6, 54; 12:24, 34, 46; 14:10, 17, 25; 15:4 (three times), 5, 6, 7 (twice), 9, 10 (twice), 16; 19:31; 21:22, 23.

[35]On this theme, see the important study of Jürgen Heise, *Bleiben: Menein in den Johanneischen Schriften* (Hermeneutische Untersuchungen zur Theologie, 8; Tübingen: Mohr, 1967).

in his Father's house (John 8:31). In the farewell discourses (John 13–17) the evangelist unfolds the true meaning of abiding for his readers. Jesus returns to the Father in order to prepare a place for his disciples so that they might be with him (John 14:2-3).

The Father abides in Jesus (John 14:10) and the Spirit abides in Jesus' disciples (John 14:17). To abide is not only to stay with; it is also to dwell in. There is, in fact, a mutual indwelling between Jesus and his disciples. They abide in him and he abides in them (John 15:4, 5, 7). The disciples abide in Jesus' love (John 15:9, 10), and his words abide in them (John 15:7).[36] Elsewhere, the evangelist informs his readers that the ultimate significance of the Eucharist is that it is the means of this mutual and life-giving indwelling. "He who eats my flesh and drinks my blood abides in me, and I in him" (John 6:56), says Jesus to his disciples in the synagogue of Capernaum.

All of this is foreshadowed when Jesus invites the paradigmatic pair of unnamed disciples to come and see where it is that he is staying. His invitation is not that the disciples should come to visit some bedouin's tent or a roadside inn; it is that they should come to perceive that Jesus abides with the Father and the Father with him. It is that they should come to experience that mutual indwelling with Jesus which is the essence of the Christian life.

Just as John had seen *(horaō)* the Spirit remain *(menō)* upon Jesus, the disciples are invited to see *(horaō)* where Jesus abides *(menō)*. In one and the other instance it is not a matter of seeing with physical eyesight; rather it is a matter of the perception that comes with faith. As John had experienced the vision that God had promised (vv. 32-34), so the disciples accept Jesus' invitation. "Come and see," he says, and they come and see. The disciples of Jesus come to perceive where it is that Jesus truly abides.

Discipleship

In this paradigm of discipleship, the evangelist offers his readers a vision of discipleship uniquely his own. He shares with the Synoptics the idea that discipleship entails radical commitment,

[36]Cf. John 5:38.

yet he vividly portrays that commitment in his own fashion. No longer does the radical decision to be a disciple entail the abandonment of secular employment in order to follow an itinerant charismatic preacher; rather, it entails the abandonment of one's prior faith commitment.

Undoubtedly this view of discipleship was consistent with the situation of the evangelist's community. Its members lived in a time when being disciples of Jesus placed them in a unique situation. Their faith commitment to Jesus gave them an identity distinct from that of the Jews and of John's disciples. Similarly consistent with the evangelist's situation years after the death and resurrection of Jesus was the notion that faith comes as the result of the testimony of another human person. However, discipleship is really a matter of responding to Jesus' invitation. Jesus' question[37] initiates the invitation; his "come and see" brings it to fulfillment.

Time is of the utmost importance in the Fourth Gospel. Not only does it serve such literary purposes as connecting disparate episodes, providing a narrative framework and imparting a dramatic flair to the tale, it also often serves to express symbolically a theological truth. We have only to think of the importance of night[38] and day and of light and darkness in the Fourth Gospel. Repeatedly the evangelist makes pointed reference to Jesus' "hour" *(hōra).* The "hour" is the time of Jesus' passion-glorification (John 2:4; 7:30; 8:20; 12:23, 27; 13:1; 16:2, 4, 21, 25, 32; 17:1).[39] In John 1:39, the "tenth hour" is not the hour of Jesus, but it is a momentous hour. As Rudolf Bultmann suggests, the tenth hour is the hour of fulfillment.[40]

---

[37] Cf. John 9:35.

[38] John 3:2; 9:4; 11:10; 13:30; 19:39.

[39] Cf. John 4:21, 23; 5:25, 28.

[40] See Rudolf Bultmann, *The Gospel of John: A Commentary* (Philadelphia: Westminster, 1971) 100. Cf. Siegfried Schulz, *Das Evangelium nach Johannes* (Das Neue Testament Deutsch, 4; Göttingen: Vandenhoeck und Ruprecht, 1972) 41.

3

Andrew

The reader of the Fourth Gospel is no doubt intrigued by the fact that the evangelist has hitherto left the disciples of Jesus in nameless anonymity. The reader would certainly like to know who the disciples are, and all the more so if he or she is familiar with the Synoptics' stories, where the first disciples to be called by Jesus are two pairs of brothers who are fishermen by trade, Peter and Andrew, James and John (Matt 4:18-22; Mark 1:16-20).

The reader's curiosity is but partially satisfied as the fourth evangelist continues his narrative. He immediately identifies one of the previously unnamed disciples as Andrew, Simon Peter's brother, but he leaves the other under a cloud of anonymity.[1] Tradition and several modern commentators think that the nameless disciple may well be the beloved disciple. Some have thought that the anonymity of the nameless disciple is an expression of humility on the part of the beloved disciple. Yet such humility does not seem characteristic of the description of the beloved disciple. The evangelist is hardly disinclined to proclaim the special love that Jesus had for this disciple and appears eager to show him as a disciple more faithful to Jesus than even Simon Peter was.[2]

Tradition has also identified the evangelist with the beloved disciple and the beloved disciple with John the son of Zebedee, whose

---

[1] See Frans Neirynck, "The Anonymous Disciple in John 1," *Ephemerides Theologicae Lovanienses* 66 (1990) 5-37.

[2] Cf. John 13:21-26; 19:25-27; 20:2-10; 21:2-7, 19-24.

name does not appear in the Fourth Gospel. Contemporary biblical scholarship is quite hesitant with regard to these identifications.[3] In any case, there is hardly any warrant for identifying the nameless one of John 1:35-39 with the son of Zebedee.[4] Indeed, if the son of Zebedee was Andrew's companion on the occasion of their call to discipleship, this would be the only time in the entire New Testament that John the son of Zebedee is paired with Andrew. Normally John is paired with his brother James,[5] and Andrew with his brother Peter,[6] as he is in John 1:40-42.

That the evangelist identifies Andrew as Simon Peter's brother is an indication that those for whom his written Gospel is intended are generally familiar with its characters. Simon Peter has not yet appeared in the evangelist's narrative, yet he is well enough known to the evangelist's readership that Peter's fraternal relationship with Andrew is sufficient identification of Andrew himself. In the tradition of the early Church, Andrew is simply Peter's brother.[7]

Although the fourth evangelist shares with the common tradition of the Church the characterization of Andrew as Peter's brother, he develops his own portrayal of the disciple.[8] In Matthew, Mark, and Luke-Acts, Andrew's name always appears on

[3]The purpose and length of the present book obviates the discussion of this complex issue. The reader will find the matter discussed at length in any of the major commentaries on the Fourth Gospel, for example, those of Barrett, Brown, Haenchen, Lindars, and Schnackenburg.

[4]Boismard suggests that it is more likely that the evangelist had Philip in mind than that he had the son of Zebedee in mind. As an argument in favor of the anonymous one being Philip, he cites the consistency of the chapter. If Andrew and Philip are the disciples of 1:35-39, the evangelist has followed up the story of their call with stories pointing to the consequences of their call, Andrew leads Peter to Jesus while Philip leads Nathanael to Jesus. Cf. M.-E. Boismard, *Moïse ou Jésus: Essai de christologie johannique* (Bibliotheca Ephemeridum Theologicarum Lovaniensium, 84; Louvain: University Press, 1988) 26.

[5]See Matthew 4:21; 10:2; 17:1; Mark 1:19, 29; 3:17; 5:37; 9:2; 10:35, 41; 13:3; 14:33; Luke 5:10; 6:14; 8:51; 9:28, 54.

[6]See Matthew 4:18; 10:2; Mark 1:16, 29; Luke 6:14. The manner of citing the two pairs of brothers in Mark 13:3 (cf. Mark 1:29; Acts 1:13) is unique in the New Testament.

[7]Matthew 4:18; 10:2; Mark 1:16 (29); Luke 6:14).

[8]Cf. Peter M. Peterson, *Andrew, Brother of Simon Peter: His History and His Legends* (Supplements to Novum Testamentum, 1; Leiden: Brill, 1958) 4-5.

a list. The list may consist of two,[9] four,[10] or twelve[11] names, but no specific function is ever attributed to Andrew. Andrew is simply the brotherly companion of Peter or one of the Twelve. Things are different in the Fourth Gospel, where Andrew is clearly portrayed as a real disciple of Jesus. He is even a disciple who has something to say. He speaks to his brother (John 1:41), and he speaks to Jesus (John 6:9).[12]

For the fourth evangelist, Andrew is a flesh-and-blood character who comes from a real city. He is a native of Bethsaida (John 1:44), a Galilean town (John 12:21).[13] That Jesus would choose his disciples from among the Galileans stands to reason, since so much of his public activity was concentrated in the Galilean region. This is the case even in the Fourth Gospel, where Jesus is often portrayed as being in Jerusalem on the occasion of festal celebrations.

The evangelist takes pains to portray Andrew as a real disciple. He presents a "thesis on discipleship" (John 1:35-39) and then illustrates his thesis with the example of Andrew. He will adopt a similar technique in chapters 2 and 3, where he portrays Jesus as knowing what lies within the human person *(anthrōpos,* John 2:25) and offers Nicodemus *(anthrōpos,* John 3:1) as a case in point.

Andrew is a disciple who has followed the full program of discipleship. He has heard testimony to Jesus. He has followed Jesus. He has offered testimony about Jesus to others. Receiving testimony to Jesus, becoming a disciple, and offering testimony about Jesus to others as an expression of one's discipleship is the normal pattern of discipleship according to the evangelist's vision of things. Just as Andrew has something to say about Jesus to his

[9]Matthew 4:18; Mark 1:16, 29.

[10]Mark 3:18; Acts 1:13.

[11]Matthew 10:2; Mark 3:13; Luke 6:14.

[12]Cf. John 12:22.

[13]Actually the town of Bethsaida belonged to the territory of Gaulinitis, but the evangelist was not alone among first-century writers in locating it in Galilee. Ptolemy and Josephus did so as well. The evangelist's identification of Bethsaida as the hometown of Andrew is different from the information provided by Mark, who locates the brothers' home in Capernaum (see Mark 1:21, 29).

brother (John 1:41), Philip has something to say about him to Nathanael (John 1:45), and the Samaritan woman has something to say about him to the natives of her town (John 4:29, 39). In this chain reaction from testimony to testimony, the gospel continues to be proclaimed and people come to believe.

The evangelist highlights the identity of Andrew as a real disciple and contributes to the drama of his narrative by telling his readers that Andrew first *(prōton)* "found his brother" (John 1:41). The very first thing this new disciple does is to find his brother and tell him about Jesus. Caught up in the movement of Jesus' disciples, Andrew has to tell someone about Jesus, and his brother Simon is the fortunate beneficiary of his testimony.

"We have found the Messiah," says Andrew to his brother. Once again, the evangelist translates a Hebrew expression into Greek for the benefit of his readers.[14] "Messiah" and "Christ" are, in Hebrew and Greek respectively, derivatives of the Hebrew and Greek verbs that have as their meaning "to anoint." Thus, "Messiah" and "Christ" mean exactly the same thing, "the Anointed One." The English-language terms[15] are perfect synonyms. They have simply come to us from different linguistic roots.

That the evangelist portrays Andrew as testifying to Jesus as the Messiah (Christ) provides confirmation that John's testimony to Jesus as the Son of God (John 1:34) was testimony to his messianic status. Through his encounter with Jesus, Andrew comes to see the truth of John's witness. Nonetheless, the evangelist writes that Andrew has found the Messiah. Earlier, Andrew had been described as one who was seeking (John 1:38); now he is presented as one who has found. The searcher has found in Jesus what he was looking for.

The reader of the Fourth Gospel should not overlook the fact that Andrew, who had initially called Jesus "Rabbi," "my teacher," now calls Jesus "Messiah," "the Anointed One." When the evangelist portrays disciples calling upon Jesus as a rabbi, he often describes those disciples as coming to Jesus and asking a

[14]Cf. John 1:38.

[15]In English, "Messiah" and "Christ" are not so much translations of the ancient Hebrew and Greek terms as they are transliterations of the Hebrew and Greek words.

question.[16] In the Jewish ambience in which the Fourth Gospel was formed, it was typical for students to come to their rabbis in order to learn from them. The fourth evangelist uses his knowledge of this practice as he describes disciples coming to Jesus, addressing him as "Rabbi," and then learning something from the one whom they have acknowledged to be their teacher.

True disciples learn from Jesus something as to who he really is. Sometimes the growth of the disciples' Christological insight is suggested by the fact that disciples who began a conversation with Jesus by addressing him as "Rabbi" exit the encounter by making a more profound Christological statement. This is the case for Andrew, just as it will be for Nathanael (John 1:49) and Mary Magdalene (John 20:16, 18).

That the evangelist considers Andrew to be a real disciple is apparent from his messianic confession of faith in Jesus. He proclaims, *"We* have found the Messiah." On the merely narrative level, the "we" makes obvious reference to Andrew and his nameless companion whose encounter with Jesus had been described in the previous scene. On a more profound level, the "we" is a Johannine "we."[17] The "we" represents the entire Johannine circle whose faith in Jesus Messiah is proclaimed in the words placed on the lips of Andrew.

Thus, in his very short description of the role of Andrew (John 1:[35-39], 40-41) the evangelist portrays Andrew as a real disciple. What is singular about his description of Andrew is that Andrew is so moved by his commitment as a disciple of Jesus that he goes and finds his brother to tell him about Jesus and bring him to Jesus. If there is one trait that is consistent in the evangelist's unique characterization of Andrew, it is that Andrew brings people to Jesus.

---

[16]John 1:38; 6:25; 9:2; 11:8.

[17]See Ch. 1 above, n. 41. John 1:41 is, nonetheless, absent from Godfrey C. Nicholson's listing of twenty-nine instances in the Fourth Gospel where "we" expresses the point of view of the evangelist's community (John 1:14, 16, 45; 3:11; 4:22, 42(?); 6:5, 68, 69; 9:4; 11:11; 14:22; 16:30; 20:25; 21:24). Cf. G. C. Nicholson, *Death as Departure: The Johannine Descent-Ascent Schema* (Society of Biblical Literature Dissertation Series, 63; Chico, Calif.: Scholars, 1983) 31.

John 6:1-15 and 12:20-26

Andrew again appears as a disciple in the story of the feeding of the five thousand (John 6:1-15). This time he is formally introduced as "one of his [Jesus'] disciples" *(heis ek tōn mathētōn autou,* John 6:8).[18] Andrew's role is to bring the young boy with the fish and the barley loaves to Jesus: "There is a lad here who has five barley loaves and two fish; but what are they among so many?" (John 6:9). Andrew's presentation of the boy to Jesus and his leading question set the stage for Jesus' revelatory gesture, the "sign" of the loaves, just as his presentation of Peter to Jesus had set the stage for Jesus' revelatory statement, "You shall be called Cephas."

In the Fourth Gospel Andrew appears yet a third time. The scene is Jerusalem, and the occasion is a feast (John 12:20-26). On that occasion Andrew joins with Philip in introducing to Jesus some Greeks who want to see Jesus. In some ways the evangelist's account seems to attribute a lesser role to Andrew than he does to Philip, yet there is consistency in his characterization of Andrew as someone who brings people to Jesus. Even Philip does not do so without the assistance of Andrew. Andrew is a real disciple, whose discipleship is realized in his confession of faith and is completed in his bringing other would-be disciples to Jesus. The Andrew of the Fourth Gospel is not simply the "other brother;" he has a specific role to play as a real disciple.

Characterization

The evangelist's characterization of Andrew as a real disciple sharply distinguishes the Fourth Gospel from the Synoptics, where Andrew appears merely as a name on a list. The Synoptic Gospels have no parallel to the evangelist's story of the encounter between Jesus and Andrew. Neither do they tell us about Andrew bringing Peter to Jesus. Nor do they tell the story of the Greeks' introduction to Jesus through the good offices of Philip and Andrew.

---

[18]Cf. "one of the two who heard . . . and followed" *(heis ek tōn duo tōn akousantōn . . . kai akolouthēsantōn)* in John 1:40.

All three Synoptic Gospels do, however, narrate the story of Jesus feeding the multitude.[19] Indeed, Matthew and Mark tell the story not once but twice. In none of these stories are any of Jesus' disciples mentioned by name. It is only in choral fashion that the disciples say: "This is a lonely place, and the hour is now late; send them away, to go into the country and villages round about and buy themselves something to eat."[20] To Jesus' command that the disciples feed the crowds, the chorus responds with the question that speaks of their reluctance: "Shall we go and buy two hundred denarii of bread and give it to them to eat?"[21] Then, when Jesus asks the disciples about the availability of bread, it is the chorus of disciples that answers: "Five, and two fish."[22]

In the Fourth Gospel, however, it is Philip who speaks of the purchase of two hundred denarii's worth of bread and of the insufficiency of that purchase for such a great crowd (John 6:7). Andrew speaks of the availability of five barley loaves and the pair of fish (John 6:8-9). The evangelist places statements which the earlier tradition had attributed to nameless disciples on the lips of specific disciples.

This flesh-and-blood quality is one of the principal features of the Fourth Gospel. The evangelist's tendency to introduce specific characters into his narrative is one of his distinctive literary techniques—individualism is characteristic of his work.[23] On the literary level, this individualism provides the Fourth Gospel's narrative with a manifest concreteness and contributes strongly to the dramatic flair that characterizes the entire narrative.

Individualism may also reflect the long homiletic tradition that lies behind the Fourth Gospel. This Gospel, like the other New Testament Gospels, was not composed by an author who retired

---

[19]Matthew 14:13-21; 15:32-39; Mark 6:32-44; 8:1-10; Luke 9:10b-17.

[20]Mark 6:35-36; parallel, Matthew 14:15; Luke 9:12.

[21]Mark 7:37. Cf. Mark 8:4; parallel, Matthew 15:33.

[22]Mark 6:38; parallel, Matthew 14:17; Luke 9:13. Cf. Mark 8:7; Matthew 15:34.

[23]Cf. R. F. Collins, "The Representative Figures of the Fourth Gospel," *Downside Review* 93 (1976), esp. pp. 26-27; *These Things Have Been Written*, 1-3; R. Alan Culpepper, *Anatomy of the Fourth Gospel: A Study in Literary Design* (New Testament Foundations and Facets; Philadelphia: Fortress, 1983) ch. 3, "Characters," 99-148.

to a studio, there to give vent to his imagination and produce a literary work. The New Testament Gospels are the end product of a long homiletic tradition in the early Church. In missionary settings and in gatherings of believers, Christian preachers told stories about Jesus. It is quite likely that in the gatherings of the Johannine circle preachers would tell their stories in dramatic fashion, citing one or another individual as a case in point. In this way, various individuals known to the Christian tradition came to represent one or another aspect of the Christian story. They acquired the status of what I have called "representative figures."[24]

The choice of a character enabled the preacher and later the evangelist to make his point in dramatic fashion. Some might find in this tendency the reflection of one or another theological conviction on the part of the evangelist and his tradition. One might, for example, cite the idea that the evangelist considers belief to be a matter of a personal faith decision or the idea that the evangelist is highlighting the significance of an individual's relationship with God in Christ. In any case, the evangelist clearly uses different characters to portray various aspects of discipleship and various ways of relating to Jesus. As a case in point, Andrew illustrates that the role of a disciple is to bring others to Jesus.

Nonetheless, there may be something more to the evangelist's portrayal of Andrew than these features that derive from the oral traditions within his circle and the evangelist's own literary techniques. It is not unlikely that the situation of the evangelist's community also contributed to the way in which he portrayed Andrew. The evangelist has, after all, effectively removed Andrew from the list of the Twelve. He has, moreover, portrayed Andrew as one who became a disciple even before his more famous brother, Simon Peter, came to believe in Jesus.

Among first-century Christians, "the Twelve" were a particularly significant group.[25] The number functioned somewhat sym-

[24]Cf. Collins, "Representative Figures," esp. pp. 29–31; *These Things Have Been Written*, 6–8.

[25]See Matthew 10:5; 26:14, 47; Mark 3:16; 4:10; 6:7; 9:35; 10:32; 11:11; 14:10, 17, 20, 43; Luke 8:1; 9:1, 12; 18:31; 22:3, 47; Acts 6:2; 1 Corinthians 15:5.

bolically. It suggested that the disciples of Jesus were the foundation of God's new people, similar to the way in which the twelve patriarchs, patronymics of the twelve tribes of Israel, were the foundation of God's people of old.[26] The symbolization corresponded to the apocalyptic outlook of the first generations of Jesus' disciples and to the later self-understanding of the early Church.

"The Twelve" play a relatively insignificant role in the Fourth Gospel. They are mentioned only in John 6:67-71 (three times)[27] and in John 20:24. In both of these passages "the Twelve" do not shine in the greatest light. In the first scene, Judas appears for the first time, identified as "one of the Twelve" *(heis ek tōn dōdeka)* and as one who will betray Jesus (John 6:71). In the second scene, Thomas is identified as "one of the Twelve" *(heis ek tōn dōdeka)* and as one who initially, at least, denies the resurrection of Jesus. It is clear that the evangelist does not put "the Twelve" in the best light.

Moreover, the fourth evangelist does not offer a list of "the Twelve" as do the Synoptics.[28] The closest the fourth evangelist comes to offering such a list is in the epilogue of his Gospel, where he describes a manifestation of the Risen Jesus to seven disciples, a markedly Johannine construction (John 21:2). Seven is a number that signifies a full complement. The evangelist's full complement does not include the Twelve as such. As a matter of fact, the evangelist does not specifically cite the ancient tradition of the appearance of the Risen Jesus to "the Twelve."[29] This tradition, however, obviously lies behind the evangelist's descriptions of the appearances of the Risen Jesus in John 20:19-29 because Thomas is identified as one of the Twelve in verse 24. Thomas is not with the other disciples when Jesus first appears to them (John 20:19-23), but he is with them at the time of the second appearance (John 20:26-29). In neither case, however, is the group

---

[26]Cf. Matthew 19:28; Luke 22:29.

[27]Cf. John 6:13.

[28]Matthew 10:2-4; Mark 3:14-19; Luke 6:13-16. Cf. Acts 1:13.

[29]1 Corinthians 15:5.

of disciples to whom Jesus appears specifically identified as the Twelve.

From these reflections one might glean the impression that the fourth evangelist is adopting a somewhat polemic attitude with regard to "the Twelve." Although "polemic" might be too strong a word to use in a reconstructed portrayal of the relationship that existed between the members of the Johannine circle and other first-century Christians, it is quite likely that some tension did exist among them. The Johannine circle seems to have led a life of Christian faith somewhat independently of other first-century Christians. Their tradition was shaped by the witness of the beloved disciple, and they seem to have existed at some distance removed from what Raymond Brown calls the "Christians of the apostolic churches."[30]

In many ways the Peter of the Fourth Gospel is a figure who represents these apostolic Christians. In his portrayal of Peter as one who is introduced to Jesus by Andrew, the fourth evangelist effectively deprives his Peter of the status of being Jesus' first disciple. Indeed he even places on the lips of Andrew the confession of Jesus as Messiah, a confession that other Christian traditions commonly attribute to Peter.[31]

The Synoptic Gospels attest to the primary status that Peter enjoyed in the apostolic Churches not only by virtue of their narration of the call of Peter before they mention the call of any other disciple but also insofar as each one of them, when offering a listing of the Twelve,[32] cites the name of Simon called Peter in the very first instance. Indeed, Matthew even designates Peter as "the first" *(protōs)* in his listing of the twelve apostles.[33] The fourth evangelist would have none of that, for he has a particular vision of the role of Peter that he would like to share with his readers.

---

[30]Cf. Raymond E. Brown, *The Community of the Beloved Disciple* (New York: Paulist, 1979) 81–88.

[31]See Matthew 16:15; Mark 8:29; Luke 9:20.

[32]Matthew 10:2; Mark 3:16; Luke 6:14. Cf. Acts 1:13; 1 Corinthians 15:5 (" . . . to Cephas, then to the twelve . . . "). Cf. John 21:2.

[33]Matthew 10:2.

4

Simon Peter

One indication that the evangelist presumes his readers to be generally familiar with the Gospel story and its characters is that he introduces a man called "Simon Peter" in John 1:40. Yet not until a couple of verses later (John 1:42), when he describes the first encounter between Jesus and Peter, does the evangelist remind his readers that the man's real name is Simon. Jesus gives to the man named Simon the honorific surname of Peter.

According to the fourth evangelist's account, Simon is introduced to Jesus by his brother Andrew, who tells Peter about the Messiah and brings him to Jesus. Thus, there is something rather ordinary about the way Simon Peter comes to Jesus. First, he benefits from the testimony of a believer who introduces him to Jesus. Then, acceptance of that testimony leads to Simon Peter's personal encounter with Jesus and to the unique relationship that he is to enjoy with Jesus. To begin, then, Simon Peter is another one of the disciples.

A New Name

There is, nevertheless, something unique about the disciple named Simon. Brought to Jesus by the messianic confession professed by his brother, Peter is addressed in mysterious fashion: "So you are Simon the son of John? You shall be called Cephas" (John 1:42). This formula, preceded by the indication that Jesus looks at Simon as he utters these strange words, is akin to the revelation formula found in John 1:29, 36, 47; 19:26-27.[1] It shares with the full formula the elements of (1) a prophetic figure (2) seeing someone and (3) saying (4) something enigmatic apropos of one who has been seen.[2] In the use of this formula, we recognize the evangelist's editorial hand at work. His hand is likewise responsible[3] for the translation of Cephas as Peter.[4]

The story the evangelist narrates also gives the impression that he is passing on a very old tradition. Andrew has spoken to Peter of Jesus as the Messiah, and now Jesus addresses Peter as Cephas. Both "Messiah" and "Cephas" are Aramaic words rarely found in the New Testament. The fourth evangelist is the only New Testament author to use "Messiah," and he does so only one other time (John 4:25). Apart from the evangelist's description of the encounter between Jesus and Simon Peter, no New Testament author except Paul,[5] the first of the New Testament writers, uses Cephas as a name for Simon Peter.

The evangelist's description of the new name given to Simon Peter serves to highlight the unique relationship that exists between Simon Peter and Jesus. The name is not only a new one for Simon; it really was a new name. With but one isolated exception, ancient literature does not offer any evidence of a person being called Cephas or Peter prior to Jesus naming Peter in this fashion. Giving this new name to Simon is, obviously, an act of authority on Jesus' part. People were entitled to name the per-

[1]See ch. 1 above, p. 28.

[2]John 1:42 lacks the presentation verb "behold" *(ide)*. In addition, the demands of the evangelist's narrative have led to the omission of "Simon" as the direct object of the verb of seeing *(emblepsas)*.

[3]The RSV's translation of John 1:42 interprets *su ei Simōn ho huios Iōannou* as a question, "So you are Simon the son of John?" If the words are to be so translated, the use of a question as an opening gambit would be another example of the evangelist's characteristic style. The ancient Greek manuscripts were, however, without punctuation and most of the modern English translations translate the words as an indicative statement, "you are Simon, the son of John" (Cf. JB, NJB, NEB, NAB, NIV, etc.).

[4]Other such translations are to be found in John 1:38, 41, 42; 4:25; 9:7; 11:16; 19:13, 17; 20:16, 24; 21:2.

[5]See 1 Corinthians 1:12; 3:22; 9:5; 15:5; Galatians 1:18; 2:9, 11, 14.

sons or things under their control,[6] and fathers gave names to their children.[7] Naming was an expression of authority.

In the Semitic world in which Jesus lived, names were not simply convenient tags by which one person could be distinguished from another. Names given to children frequently were an expression of their parent's faith, as was the case for John ("God has mercy"). Often names served to indicate one's role in life.[8] In any event, names were considered to be closely related to the person who bore them—a virtual manifestation of the person who carried them. As a result, names were not changed as easily as they are in our modern world. To change a name almost implied a change in one's identity; certainly it implied a change in one's role in life. Thus the biblical tradition preserves the memory of the change of Abram's name to Abraham[9] and that of Jacob to Israel.[10] These name changes were not only acts of authority on the part of Yahweh vis-à-vis the patriarchs; they also symbolized the role in the formation of his people that Yahweh accorded to these heroes of the Jewish tradition.

All four of the Gospels in the New Testament draw attention to the importance of Simon's new name.[11] Nonetheless, readers generally think of the story found in Matthew 16:15-19 when they think of the change of Simon's name:

> He said to them, "But who do you say that I am?" Simon Peter replied, "You are the Christ, the Son of the living God." And Jesus answered him, "Blessed are you, Simon Bar-Jona! For flesh and blood has not revealed this to you, but my Father who is in heaven. And I tell you, you are Peter, and on this rock I will build my church, and the powers of death shall not prevail against it. I will give you the keys of the kingdom of

---

[6]See, for example, Genesis 2:20; Daniel 1:7.

[7]Cf. Matthew 1:25; Luke 1:63.

[8]Cf. Matthew 1:21. The name "Jesus" (Joshua) means "Yahweh saves."

[9]Genesis 17:5.

[10]Genesis 32:38; 35:10.

[11]See Matthew 10:2. "Simon, who is called Peter"; Mark 3:16, "Simon whom he surnamed Peter"; and Luke 6:14, "Simon, whom he named Peter."

heaven, and whatever you bind on earth shall be bound in heaven, and whatever you loose on earth shall be loosed in heaven."

In comparison with this relatively long scene described by Matthew, the fourth evangelist's narrative is very sparse indeed. Indeed, it is more akin to the brief mention of the name change found in Matthew 10:2, "Simon, who is called Peter"; Mark 3:16, "Simon whom he surnamed Peter"; and Luke 6:14, "Simon, whom he named Peter" than it is to the relatively long story of Matthew 16. While it is true that the fourth evangelist presents a scenario for the name change, it is a scenario that is clearly of his own creation and one that fits in well with the style of the first chapter of his Gospel.

The evangelist does not speculate on the significance of the change of name. Nor does he attempt to offer any popular etymology as a clue to its meaning. He simply translates the new Aramaic name "Cephas" by an equally new Greek name "Peter" *(Petros)*. There is no mention of the rock and still less of a church built on a rock. There is no further ecclesiological reflection, nor is there any speculation on the role of Peter as a doorkeeper with the power of the keys.

For the evangelist, the new name, Peter, is clearly a surname. In the evangelist's world the nomenclature would have been quite strange. It was the usual custom to distinguish, when necessary, one "Simon" from another or one "Judas" from another by adding a patronymic reference, as the evangelist himself does in John 1:42; 6:71; and 13:2, 26.[12] For the evangelist Simon's new name was indeed important. Each time the evangelist mentions Simon's name, he adds the honorific surname Peter[13]—that is, with the exception of John 1:41 and 42, where the name "Simon" appears

---

[12]Cf. John 1:45; 6:42. The Aramaic word for "son" is *bar* (cf. Matt 16:17). As a result, a number of composite patronymic names appear in the New Testament, for example, Barabbas (Mark 15:7), Bartholomew (Mark 3:18), Bar-Jesus (Acts 13:6), Barnabas (Acts 4:36), Barsabbas (Acts 1:23), and Bartimaeus (Mark 10:46).

[13]See John 1:41; 6:8, 68; 13:6, 9, 24, 36; 18:10, 15, 25; 20:2, 6; 21:2, 3, 7, 11, 15. An exception to the general rule is to be found in the post-resurrectional dialogue found in John 21:15-17. As a form of direct address in the story, Jesus simply calls Simon "Simon" when he asks about the latter's love for him.

without the addition of "Peter." At this point in the story, however, the omission of the name "Peter" is almost inevitable, precisely because the evangelist is about to recall that it was Jesus
who gave the additional name of Peter to the man called Simon.
In the Fourth Gospel there are also a few times when the evangelist simply uses the surname Peter,[14] without mentioning that
the man's given name is Simon.

The Spokesperson

Who is this man enigmatically called Cephas? He is a brother
of Andrew and clearly one of the disciples of Jesus. In the Fourth
Gospel, he next appears in a little scene (John 6: 66-71) that is
described shortly after Jesus' long address on the bread of life
in the synagogue of Capernaum (John 6:35-58). Jesus' disciples
are divided among themselves and some are refusing to follow
him any longer. In a scene reminiscent of the Synoptics' story
of Jesus' questioning his disciples in the environs of Caesarea
Philippi,[15] Jesus asks the Twelve, "Do you also wish to go away?"

In the Fourth Gospel as in the Synoptics, the attitude of others
toward Jesus serves as the background to Jesus' pointed question. In the Synoptics the disciples tell Jesus what others are saying about him; in the Fourth Gospel the defection of some of
Jesus' disciples provides the backdrop for the interrogation. In
the Synoptics the question addressed to the disciples is "Who do
you say that I am?"[16] In the Fourth Gospel Jesus' question is "Do
you also wish to go away?" (John 6:67). In a way, both questions can almost be reduced to one—that of the disciples' identity.
Are they like the rest of men? Or is their relationship with Jesus
of a different sort?

In the Synoptics and the Fourth Gospel alike, Jesus' question
is phrased in the second person plural: who do you say *(legete)?;*
do you also wish *(thelete)* to go away? Thus it is addressed gener-

---

[14]See John 1:44; 13:37; 18:11, 16 (twice), 17, 18, 26, 27; 20:3, 4; 21:7 (twice), 17, 20, 21
in addition to "Peter" given as a translation in John 1:42.

[15]Matthew 16:13-16; Mark 8:27-29; Luke 9:18-20.

[16]Matthew 16:15; Mark 8:29; Luke 9:20.

ally to the group. The group is identified as "the disciples" in the Synoptics' account and as "the Twelve" in the Fourth Gospel's narrative. In each instance, however, it is Simon Peter who responds in the name of the group. In the Synoptics, he effectively serves as the spokesperson for the disciples. In the Fourth Gospel, he is the spokesperson for the Twelve.

Simon Peter's role as a spokesperson is presented with more clarity in the Fourth Gospel than it is in the Synoptics. In both cases Peter is the only one to respond to the general question. In the Fourth Gospel, however, Peter's response is phrased in the first person plural: "Lord, to whom shall we go? You have the words of eternal life; and we have believed, and have come to know, that you are the Holy One of God" (John 6:68-69). In the dialogue and in the confession of faith, the reader recognizes the presence of the Johannine "we."[17] Peter professes not the messianic confession of faith that had earlier been found on his brother's lips (John 1:41) but the faith of the evangelist's own community. In this respect, the faith of Simon Peter is at one with the faith of the evangelist and his circle. They share a common faith in Jesus.

The opening question in the Johannine scenario, "Do you also wish to go away?" and the interrogatory response, "Lord, to whom shall we go?" are characteristic features of the evangelist's narrative style. So, too, is the progression from Peter's "Sir," with its relatively low Christology, to his "Holy One of God," with its relatively high Christology. Within the Fourth Gospel Jesus is characteristically presented as a revealer,[18] indeed as the only revealer.[19] Eternal life is one of the major themes of the Fourth Gospel. The evangelist writes about eschatological life some thirty-six times,[20] while, together, the Synoptics mention

[17]"To whom shall *we* go [*apeleusometha*] . . . *we* have believed [*pepisteukamen*] and have come to know [*egnōkamen*]." See ch. 3 above, n. 16.

[18]This is patently clear in the bread of life discourse as it is in most of the major discourses of the Gospel. The point is also well made in the prologue's characterization of Jesus as the Word, as it is in the concluding words of the prologue: "He has made him known" (John 1:18).

[19]Cf. John 3:13, etc.

[20]See John 3:15, 16, 36; 4:14, 36; 5:24, 39; 6:27, 40, 47, 54; 10:28; 12:25, 50; 17:2, 3, as

eternal life only fourteen times. The credal lemma "we have believed" *(pepisteukamen),* introduced with an emphatic "we" *(hēmeis,* literally, "we ourselves") makes use of a verb that occurs more frequently in the Fourth Gospel than in any other New Testament text. Of the 243 occurrences of *pisteuō,* "to believe," in the New Testament, 98 are to be found in the Fourth Gospel. Finally, the expression "come to know" *(egnōkamen)* represents a use of the verb "to know" *(ginōskō)* in order to identify the insight that comes with faith.

In sum, Peter's confession of faith truly is formulated in the language of the evangelist's own circle. The Peter of John 6:68 speaks the faith of the evangelist's community.[21] He calls Jesus "Lord" and proclaims him to be the Holy One of God.[22] Peter's proclamation recalls the descriptive epithet applied to such men consecrated to God as were Aaron and Samson in the Jewish tradition.[23] It anticipates Jesus' description of himself as one sanctified[24] by the Father (John 10:36).

In some ways the little scene in which Peter appears as a spokesperson for the Twelve serves as a vehicle for the evangelist's own reflection on the Twelve. In any case, John 6:67-71 is virtually the only place in the Gospel in which the evangelist explicitly considers the Twelve.[25] The repeated mention of "the Twelve" *(hoi dōdeka)* in verses 67 and 71 identifies the little section as a literary unit. This literary technique of inclusion defines the unit and incorporates its content within a coherent whole.

The evangelist notes that the Twelve have been chosen by Jesus (John 6:70), yet the occasion and circumstances of that choice are nowhere indicated in his Gospel. Because of their fidelity to

---

well as 6:68. Cf. M.-E. Boismard, *Moïse ou Jésus: Essai de christologie johannique* (Bibliotheca Ephemeridum Theologicarum Lovaniensium, 84; Louvain: University Press, 1988) 69.

[21]This is not the only time in the Fourth Gospel that the evangelist expresses his community's point of view by means of a character in the narrative. See also John 1:41, 45; 4:42; 14:22; 16:30; 20:25.

[22]Cf. Mark 1:24; Luke 4:34.

[23]For Aaron, see Judges 13:7; 16:17; For Samson, see Psalm 106:16.

[24]That is , "made holy" *hēgiasen).*

[25]Apart from this little scene, "the Twelve" are mentioned only in John 20:24. See above, pp. 54–55.

Jesus, the Twelve stand in contrast to disciples who defect. Unlike those disciples who go away, the Twelve remain with Jesus. For them, there is no other place to go. Peter serves as the spokesperson of their common conviction when he says to Jesus: "Lord, to whom shall we go? You have the words of eternal life" (John 6:68).

One other single figure stands out within the group of the Twelve. That is Judas,[26] specifically identified as "one of the Twelve" (John 6:70).[27] He is the betrayer. His belonging to the Twelve serves to underscore the heinousness of his crime.[28] From the evangelist's point of view, however, that Judas belongs to the Twelve also serves to suggest that the group of the Twelve, initially faithful to Jesus, can not serve as a model of faith. One of them is to betray Jesus; another (John 20:24) has doubts about his resurrection. They had initially walked faithfully with Jesus, but they are to be found wanting at the end.

As the spokesperson and representative figure of the Twelve, Simon Peter portrays the ambivalence present within the group of the Twelve. Apart from Jesus, no other character in the Fourth Gospel is as richly portrayed as is Simon Peter. He is a figure of contrasts and ambivalence, indeed, a highly complex character[29] who represents the ambivalence with which the evangelist himself regarded the group of the Twelve. Historically they were important, and they would acquire increased ascendancy in various Christian communities of the first century, but they could not quite model the perfection of faith to which the evangelist was calling the community for which his Gospel was intended.[30]

---

[26]See R. F. Collins, "The Representative Figures of the Fourth Gospel," *Downside Review* 93 (1976) 118-20, *These Things Have Been Written,* 28-30; R. Alan Culpepper, *Anatomy of the Fourth Gospel: A Study in Literary Design* (New Testament Foundations and Facets; Philadelphia: Fortress, 1983) 124-25.

[27]Cf. John 12:4, where Judas is called "one of his disciples" *(heis ek tōn mathētōn).*

[28]Note not only the "one of the twelve" in v. 71, but also the "one of you" *(ex humōn heis)* in v. 70.

[29]See Culpepper, *Anatomy,* 120.

[30]On Peter in the Fourth Gospel, cf. Arthur H. Maynard, "The Role of Peter in the Fourth Gospel," *New Testament Studies* 30 (1984) 531-48.

Peter: A Contrast with Judas

In the evangelist's portrayal of the Twelve in the little scene after Jesus' instruction in the synagogue of Capernaum, Simon Peter stands in sharp contrast with Judas. What a contrast! Peter, the son of John,[31] is the spokesperson for a group of disciples who are distinguished by their fidelity to Jesus. They are so unlike those who have gone away. As a person of faith, Peter articulates the faith of the evangelist's own circle. In contrast, Judas, the son of Simon Iscariot, is a devil. He does not go away. His crime is worse. He is "the betrayer."[32]

At dinner

The evangelist again takes up the theme of Jesus' betrayal in John 13:2-11, a short unit set off as a distinct pericope within the narrative by the betrayal motif (vv. 2, 10b-11). As the evangelist mulls over Jesus' impending betrayal, he once again subtly contrasts Simon Peter with Judas, the son of Simon Iscariot. When the disciples gather together with Jesus for his farewell dinner, the evangelist reminds his readers that "the devil had already put it into the heart of Judas . . . to betray him" (John 13:2). With the gesture of washing his disciples' feet, the evangelist's Jesus symbolizes the offering of himself in death. The foot washing recalls the anointing of Jesus' feet for burial.[33] Peter clearly misunderstands the nature of Jesus' gesture (John 13:7) and impetuously refuses to have his feet washed. He is a typical disciple who misunderstands the significance of Jesus' revelatory words and symbolic gestures. Within the narrative Peter functions as a representative of the other disciples,[34] yet he is one who does not grasp the meaning of Jesus' impending death.[35]

---

[31]See John 1:42.

[32]*ho paradidous.* See John 18:2, 5. Cf. John 12:4, "he who was to betray him" *(ho mellon auton paradidonai),* inserted into the text as a Johannine note.

[33]See John 12:3, 7. Cf. Herold Weiss, "Foot Washing in the Johannine Community," *Novum Testamentum* 21 (1979) 298-325, pp. 312-14.

[34]See, especially, the emphatic plural in John 13:10b, *"you* are clean." Cf. Rudolf Schnackenburg, *The Gospel According to St. John, Vol. 3. Commentary on Chapters 13-21.* (New York: Crossroad, 1987) 22.

[35]The foot-washing scene, found only in the Fourth Gospel, may well represent a broadly

A conversation

In the subsequent discourse, Jesus picks up on the motif of his betrayal. "One of you *(heis ex humōn),*"[36] he says, "will betray me" (John 13:21). Peter replies, "Tell us of whom it is he speaks" (John 13:24). The words capture the curiosity of the entire group of disciples. Peter effectively serves as their spokesperson. Yet his words are not addressed to Jesus himself; they are rather addressed to the beloved disciple, who is here portrayed as being more intimately united to Jesus than is Peter. The beloved disciple conveys to Jesus the desire of the group, previously articulated by Simon Peter. Jesus responds with the dramatic gesture of dipping a piece of food into the liquid mixture and presenting it to Judas. Jesus himself has set the stage for the drama of the event by announcing: "It is he to whom I shall give this morsel when I have dipped it" (John 13:26). When he does so, he identifies the betrayer and satisfies, undoubtedly with relief, the curiosity of the entire group of disciples. One of them is indeed the betrayer, and that one is Judas. Peter articulates the desire of the disciples to know about the betrayer. In ignorance, he says, "Tell us of whom it is he speaks." His own lack of knowledge as to the identity of the betrayer effectively serves to contrast Simon Peter, thus distanced from the betrayal, with the betrayer himself.

In the garden

Peter and Judas appear together with Jesus in yet a third scene in the Fourth Gospel. The scene is Jesus' arrest in the garden (John 18:1-11). Once again, the treacherous betrayal of Jesus serves as the background for the narrative. The author's emphasis is readily apparent. His story line tells the tale of a motley band of soldiers and officers from the chief priests and Pharisees who have come to the garden in order to seize Jesus by force, but who, ironically, discover that absolutely no force is necessary.[37] Jesus, fully

construed Johannine parallel to the Synoptics' description of the disciples misunderstanding of Jesus' death, a scene in which Peter also serves in a representative capacity (Matt 16:21-22; Mark 8:31-32).

[36]Cf. John 6:70.

[37]Cf. R. F. Collins, "The Search for Jesus: Reflections on the Fourth Gospel," *Laval théologique et philosophique* 34 (1978) 45–47; in *These Things Have Been Written,* 122–25.

in control of the situation, willingly—and repeatedly—identifies himself for the benefit of the stupefied group and fully consents to accept his fate.

The fourth evangelist's account of Jesus' arrest is quite a different story from that found in the Synoptic Gospels (Matt 26:47-56; Mark 14:43-52; Luke 22:47-53). Their narratives do not portray a Jesus in such control that he willingly identifies himself for the benefit of those who have come out to arrest him. Those narratives (Matt 26:56; Mark 14:50-52) show the disciples fleeing in fear; the fourth evangelist's account portrays Jesus ordering that his disciples be allowed to leave (John 18:8).

Peter's lack of understanding

One of the ways in which the Fourth Gospel's story of Jesus' arrest differs from that of the Synoptics is in the introduction of named characters. It is one of the evangelist's favorite compositional techniques to cite personal names in his stories. Now, in a little scene reminiscent of a parallel story in the Synoptics (Matt 26:51-54; Mark 14:47; Luke 22:49-51), the fourth evangelist tells his readers that it is Simon Peter who has struck off the right ear of Malchus, a slave belonging to the high priest.

The mention of the names of Peter and Malchus are typical of the fourth evangelist's narrative.[38] Along with the precision of the *right* ear,[39] they provide his account with a realism and a dramatic effect absent from the anonymous tale told by the Synoptics. The use of a question (v. 11) and the double name Simon Peter are characteristic of the fourth evangelist's personal style. That he introduces Simon Peter into an account that another tradition passes along in nameless fashion is rather important.

Jesus' statement to Peter, "Put your sword into its sheath," harkens back to a dialogue that was part of the farewell discourse. Then, the headstrong Peter professed his readiness to follow Jesus

[38]Cf. John 6:5-9.

[39]See, nonetheless, Luke 22:50 as compared with Matthew 26:51 and Mark 14:47. The precise reference to the right ear found in John and Luke is one of several incidental details which are common to both of these evangelists. One might note, however, that the fourth evangelist does not share Luke's concern that the soldier be healed (Luke 22:51). His own agenda in the description of the garden scene is quite different from Luke's.

until the end. Peter vigorously proclaimed that he was ready to lay down his life,[40] even as Jesus had proclaimed his readiness to lay down his life for those who were his own (John 10:11, 15, 17, 18). Now, in the garden, when Jesus is on the point of laying down his life, Peter takes up the sword.

The armed Peter, ready to defend Jesus at the critical moment, stands in marked contrast with Judas, who has come out to the garden in the company of an armed band of soldiers and officers. The one is the betrayer; the other, the defender. The betrayer is silent. He has nothing to say and Jesus has nothing to say to him. Peter, too, is silent. Yet Jesus tells Peter, equivalently at least, that his hour is at hand and that he is ready: "Shall I not drink the cup which the Father has given me?" (John 18:11b).

As Peter is contrasted subtly but ever so surely with Judas, the reader of the fourth evangelist's story realizes that all is not copacetic as far as Peter is concerned. When Jesus says, "Put your sword into its sheath" (John 18:11a), Peter receives a mild rebuke. At this critical moment Simon Peter's way is not Jesus' way. Jesus is to drink the cup that the Father has given him; Peter's headstrong gesture is opposed to the path set out by the Father.

Peter had professed his willingness to follow Jesus (John 13:37); now he seems unwilling to allow Jesus to go his way. In the discussion about the washing of feet (John 13:6-10) and in the dialogue of John 13:36-38, conversations that clearly bear the marks of the evangelist's own compositional techniques, Simon Peter is portrayed as one who does not really comprehend the true significance of Jesus' impending hour. Now, in the garden, he gives dramatic expression to his lack of comprehension. Peter is someone who does not fully understand the nature of Jesus' own hour. Simon Peter may be contrasted with Judas, who has betrayed Jesus, but he really doesn't understand what the passion of Jesus is all about.

The Synoptic authors tell the story of Peter's confession of faith in Jesus as the Messiah (Matt 16:16; Mark 8:29; Luke 9:20), but Peter's moment of glory is short-lived. Expecting Jesus to be the political and military leader eagerly awaited by much of the Jew-

---

[40] *Tithēmi tēn psuchēn;* John 13:37, 38.

ish population, Peter is not willing to accept the idea of a Christ who would suffer, be killed, and only then be raised from the dead (Matt 16:21-22; Mark 8:31-32).[41] Because he does not understand what it really means for Jesus to be king, Peter is sharply rebuked. "Get behind me, Satan! For you are not on the side of God, but of men," is what Peter hears from Jesus' lips (Mark 8:33; Matt 16:23).

In the Fourth Gospel, Peter continues to appear as one who does not understand what is really going on as far as Jesus' passion is concerned. Jesus kingship is the focal theme of the Fourth Gospel's passion narrative.[42] What does it mean for Jesus to be the Messiah-king? Peter does not perceive the real nature of Jesus' kingship. Rather, he thinks in the worldly political-military categories that Jesus rejects as the key to the correct understanding of his kingship (John 18:36). Misunderstanding the nature of Jesus' kingship and misunderstanding, along with this, the nature of Jesus' hour, Peter suffers a mild rebuke when Jesus tells him to put his sword away.

Peter: A Contrast with the Beloved Disciple

If in John 6:67-71; 13:21-30; and 18:1-11 Simon Peter appears as the antithesis of Judas, the son of Simon Iscariot, he also stands in contrast to the enigmatic figure of the beloved disciple, introduced into the Fourth Gospel's narrative at John 13:23. This abrupt introduction of a hitherto unmentioned character just as the story is about to reach its climax—indeed, when Jesus is portrayed as gathering with his own for a farewell meal and final instructions (the "farewell discourse," John 13-17)—would be surprising were it not that the evangelist presumes his readers to be generally familiar with the events he is about to relate. Thus, while the beloved disciple is a new character for the modern reader who takes up the Fourth Gospel for the first time, he would not have been unknown to the members of the Johannine circle for whom this Gospel was originally intended.

---

[41]Cf. Luke 9:22.
[42]Cf. John 18:33-38; 19:12-22; etc.

At this time of particular intimacy between Jesus and his disciples, the beloved disciple is portrayed as having an intimacy with Jesus that goes beyond that generally enjoyed by the group of disciples. The disciple remains unnamed and will remain unnamed throughout the Gospel. Nonetheless, his intimacy with Jesus is both explicitly stated and dramatically suggested. He is the disciple whom Jesus loves, the one lying close to the breast of Jesus *(en tō kolpō tou Iēsou).*[43] This kind of intimacy with Jesus is reminiscent of the kind of intimacy that Jesus enjoys with the Father: Jesus, beloved by the Father (John 15:9; 18:26), is the only Son, who is in the bosom of the Father *(ho hōn eis ton kolpon tou patros,* John 1:18).

The greater intimacy which this disciple enjoys with Jesus indicates that he is the one to whom Peter must turn when he wants to express the disciples' concern as to the identity of the betrayer. The beloved disciple can then say to Jesus: "Lord, who is it?" (John 13:25). The contrast between the beloved disciple and Peter is sharp enough. Peter can serve as the spokesperson for the disciples, but it is the beloved disciple who enjoys the degree of intimacy with Jesus that allows an answer to their question to be forthcoming.

In the court of the high priest

As the passion narrative moves toward its denouement in the revelation of Jesus' glory, the beloved disciple and Simon Peter appear once again as a pair when they follow Jesus to the court of the high priest (John 18:15-18). The beloved disciple appears here as "the other disciple," but there can be no doubt that the evangelist intends his readers to see in this other disciple the beloved disciple.[44] He and Simon Peter are clearly portrayed as disciples; the evangelist describes them as following Jesus.

The emphasis is upon Peter, for the verb "to follow" is in the singular *(ēkolouthei).* The reader will surely recognize in the evan-

[43]Cf. John 21:20.

[44]See my "Representative Figures," 129, *These Things Have Been Written,* 42, and the convincing demonstration offered by Frans Neirynck in "The 'Other Disciple' in Jn 18, 15-16," in *Evangelica* (Bibliotheca Ephemeridum Theologicarum Lovaniensium, 60; Louvain: University Press, 1982) 335–64.

gelist's presentation of the two disciples, with the words "and so did another disciple" *(kai allos mathētēs)* introduced almost as an add-on,[45] that the evangelist is about to rehearse another aspect of his topic. He has featured Peter and is about to write about Peter's denial. Peter is treated with mild irony when the evangelist portrays the beloved disciple as the one who enables Peter to follow Jesus into the court of the high priest. His intervention facilitates the dramatic scene in which Peter not once but three times denies Jesus (John 18:17-18; 25-27). Peter is a disciple, yet he is one who denies Jesus.

This is but one of the several ironic passages in the Fourth Gospel that highlight the figure of Peter.[46] His outward appearance is that of the faithful disciple; the reality is otherwise because he fails the test of real discipleship. He is ready to follow Jesus even to the point of laying down his life, but he takes up the sword. Nonetheless, even that dramatic manifestation of Peter's bravado is deceptive. Peter is bold in the garden, but he will deny his garden appearance (John 18:26).[47] He is a disciple, but he will deny Jesus.

At the tomb

Yet another scene in which Simon Peter appears to fail the test of discipleship is described by the evangelist in John 20:2-10. Once again, Simon Peter and the beloved disciple are paired together. From the lips of Mary Magdalene they hear a startling announcement: "They have taken the Lord out of the tomb, and we do not know where they have laid him" (John 20:2). The pair of disciples react immediately and vigorously. They run to the tomb. There the beloved disciple defers to Peter: Although he has arrived at the tomb before Peter, he allows Peter to enter the tomb first.

Although the evangelist is obviously composing his own narrative, he is also following an old tradition that preserves the mem-

---

[45]Cf. John 1:36; 18:15; 20:26.

[46]See Culpepper, *Anatomy,* 164–49, 174–75.

[47]This is another example of the evangelist's use of a flashback technique.

ory of Peter as the first disciple to make an inspection of the empty tomb. Luke 24:12 records that "Peter rose and ran to the tomb; stooping and looking in, he saw the linen cloths by themselves."[48] Luke goes on to state that "he [Peter] went home wondering at what had happened" (v. 12b). Apparently the sight of the empty tomb is not enough to convince Peter that Jesus has been raised.

The fourth evangelist shares with Luke the notion that Peter has not been convinced by his inspection of an empty tomb, but his presentation of Peter's lack of faith is more subtle than Luke's straightforward announcement of Peter's wonderment at the sight of the empty tomb. The fourth evangelist does not tell us that Peter has failed to believe. He tells us only that the beloved disciple "saw and believed" (John 20:8). The verbs are characteristic of the evangelist, but each of them is in the singular, which stands in grammatical contrast to the plural found in the verses that come before ("they went . . . they both ran") and after ("they did not know the scripture"). Two disciples have gone to the tomb; only one comes away as a believer. That one is the beloved disciple. Compared with him, Simon Peter is a man lacking in faith.[49]

In sum, the comparison between Simon Peter and the beloved disciple is somewhat odious as far as Peter is concerned. Each time the two disciples are paired, Peter's faith pales in comparison with that of the beloved disciple. Peter is a disciple, but there is something lacking in his discipleship. Indeed, when the fourth evangelist wants to show the ironic quality of discipleship, the contrast between the appearance and the reality, the gap between the rhetoric and the facts, he seems to feature Peter.

---

[48] The verse is missing from ancient manuscripts of the Western textual tradition. Hence it is not found in some modern translations of the Gospel, e.g., the RSV and the NEB, where the verse is cited only as a footnote.

[49] Cf. John Dominic Crossan, who writes that the evangelist lets "Peter enter the tomb first but demolishes this precendence beforehand by having the Beloved Disciple get there and look in first and demolishes it afterwards by having only the Beloved Disciple come to faith by the experience." *Four Other Gospels: Shadows on the Contours of Canon* (Minneapolis: Winston, 1985) 163.

The Epilogue

The somewhat less-than-ideal portrait of Peter found in the three scenes in the Fourth Gospel where Peter and the beloved disciple are paired together (John 13:22-25; 18:15-18; 20:2-10) is somewhat rectified by two scenes in the epilogue to the Fourth Gospel, where Simon Peter and the beloved disciple again appear as a pair.

The first scene is the rather complex story of the miraculous catch of fish (John 21:4-14), which literary analysis reveals to be a compilation of earlier stories.[50] The story focuses on Peter, who is introduced as a fisherman (John 21:3). The as-yet-unrecognized Jesus invites the disciples—that is, Peter and the disciples who have accompanied him on the fishing trip (v. 3b)—to cast their nets over the right side of the boat so that they might find some fish. The disciples do as the unknown figure suggests and catch an extremely large quantity of fish in their nets.

At this point, Simon Peter and the beloved disciple are introduced as the fourth evangelist's classic pair: "That disciple whom Jesus loved said to Peter, 'It is the Lord!' When Simon Peter heard that it was the Lord, he put on his clothes, for he was stripped for work, and sprang into the sea" (John 21:7). It is the beloved disciple who first recognizes the Risen Lord, just as it was he who had come to faith when he saw the empty tomb (John 20:8). The beloved disciple affirms the paschal proclamation, "It is the Lord." The headstrong Peter jumps into the sea—not, however, without first attending to his proper attire—apparently in order to reach Jesus as quickly as possible.[51]

The evangelist's portrayal of Peter remains consistent. Simon Peter is someone who comes to faith as a result of another disciple's testimony. Andrew had testified to Jesus-Messiah (John 1:41), and Peter had become a disciple of Jesus. The beloved dis-

---

[50]See, for example, Boismard, *Moïse ou Jésus,* 48-50.

[51]The evangelist has, however, not specified the reason for Peter's plunge into the sea. In vv. 10-11 he portrays Jesus as speaking to the disciples and Peter, apparently nearby, as the one who responded to Jesus' command. The hard connection, technically, an aporia, is one of the many indications that a complex literary history lies behind the evangelist's present account.

ciple testifies to Jesus-Lord (John 21:7), and Peter comes to belief in the Risen One. As a disciple of Jesus, Peter had served as spokesperson for the Twelve. He alone had responded to the question Jesus had asked of the Twelve (John 6:67-69). When the disciples encounter the Risen One, Peter acts on their behalf. Of the entire company of fishermen, Simon Peter alone responds when Jesus commands that some of the recently caught fish be brought to him (John 21:10-11).

The final scene in the Fourth Gospel in which Peter and the beloved disciple are paired together is the final scene in the Gospel itself. It continues to evince the tension—or friendly rivaly?—that the evangelist constantly portrays as existing between Peter and the beloved disciple.

The challenge addressed to Peter to have faith in the Risen One is summed up in the Risen Jesus' invitation, "Follow me" (John 21:19). This is the only time in the New Testament's Gospel tradition that the Risen Jesus is portrayed as calling his disciples in this fashion. Undoubtedly it is a characterization intended to show that Peter is indeed called to follow the Risen One. Jesus' invitation rehabilitates Simon Peter as a disciple.

The Risen Jesus intimates that the path of Peter's discipleship will lead to his death.[52] Ironically, Peter's desire to follow Jesus (John 6:37) means that his death will, in a fashion similar to that of Jesus' own death,[53] also glorify God (John 21:19). Nonetheless, in a final reflection on Peter's discipleship, the evangelist portrays Peter as inquiring about the fate of the beloved disciple. Even after having come to faith in the Risen One and having thus renewed his discipleship, Peter continues to exist in some state of tension with the beloved disciple. "What about this man?" says Peter to the Risen Lord. The question can hardly be taken as a sign of Peter's concern for the beloved disciple. Perhaps it is a question prompted by jealousy. In any case, it earns for Peter yet another mild rebuke from Jesus.[54] To the end, Peter remains

---

[52]On the proverbial saying found in John 21:18, see my "Proverbial Sayings in St. John's Gospel," *Melita Theologica* 37 (1986) 42–58, pp. 46–49, in *These Things Have Been Written*, 128–50, pp. 134–37.

[53]Cf. John 17:1.

[54]Cf. John 13:8, 18; 18:11.

a disciple who does not fully understand the nature of his own discipleship.

The Risen Lord nonetheless intends precisely that Peter attend to the demands of his own discipleship: "If it is my will that he remain until I come, what is that to you?" (John 21:22a.). The rebuke gently suggests[55] that Peter mind his own business. What is that business? It is that Peter be a disciple. The final words of the Risen Jesus to Peter and, indeed, the final words of the Risen Jesus—at least in the fourth evangelist's narrative—are an emphatic "Follow me!"[56] The Peter portrayed by the evangelist has been called to be a disciple.

Subtly contrasted with Judas and even more dramatically with the beloved disciple, the Peter who appears in the Fourth Gospel is one who represents the disciples of Jesus in the ambiguity of their discipleship. This alone contributes much to the complexity of the evangelist's portrait of Peter. From the standpoint of literary criticism, the evangelist's Peter is clearly a round figure.[57]

The Primacy

The figure of Peter also appears in a singularly majestic scene in the epilogue to the Fourth Gospel. This scene is sandwiched between the story of the wondrous catch of fish with its contrast between Peter and the beloved disciple (John 21:7)—to which the story of the lakeshore meal has been added—and the dialogue between Jesus and Peter on the respective fates of Peter and the beloved disciple.

The story of Peter's primacy focuses on a three-part, rather repetitive dialogue between Jesus and Simon Peter. The Risen Lord addresses Peter in a way reminiscent of the way that Peter

---

[55]The phrase, "what is that to you?" *(ti pros se)*, is classic. Cf. "what have you to do with me?" *(ti emoi kai soi;* John 2:4).

[56]In Greek the emphasis is achieved by the use of the second person singular pronoun *su* in v. 22. The emphatic pronoun is not found in v. 19, where the "follow me" is formulated in the classic manner.

[57]As distinct from a "flat figure," one that embodies a single trait. The terminology comes from Edward Morgan Forster, *Aspects of the Novel* (reprinted, New York: Penguin, 1962) 73, 81.

was addressed when he first encountered Jesus, that is, "Simon, son of John."[58] The portrayal of the Risen Lord's questioning of Peter is consistent with the way in which the fourth evangelist uses questions, especially when he shows Jesus asking questions of those with whom he will enter into a special relationship. Rather than being monotonous,[59] the triple interrogation contributes to the dramatic effect of the story.

In the epilogue to the Gospel, the evangelist frequently harkens back to the earlier narrative. The description of the beloved disciple (John 21:20) is a flashback to the farewell meal (John 13:23-35). Nowhere, however, is this recall of earlier motifs done with greater dramatic technique than in the three-fold interrogation of Peter by Jesus. The three questions correspond to the triple denial of Jesus by a Peter who, unabashedly, had denied Jesus and his own discipleship three times (John 18:17, 25, 27). In a narrative where topographical references are introduced so effectively, the presence of the charcoal fire (John 21:9) subtly recalls the charcoal fire beside which Peter was standing as he denied Jesus (John 18:18; see John 18:25).[60]

The triple interrogation is directed to Peter, upon whom the emphasis lies. Identified in the Fourth Gospel's typical nomenclature as "Simon Peter," Peter is addressed as Simon, son of John, by Jesus who asks, "Do you love me more than these?" These others then disappear from the scene. Peter avows his love for the Lord but makes no mention of the others. Neither does Jesus mention them when he questions Peter a second time about his love. Again Peter replies in stereotypical fashion, "Yes, Lord, you know that I love you" (John 21:15, 16). When Jesus asks

---

[58]The formulae of John 1:42 and 21:15, 16, 17 are not identical. John 1:42 has the full address, *Simōn ho huios Iōannou* (literally, "Simon the son of John), whereas John 21 has an elliptical *Simōn Iōannou* (literally, "Simon of John") in all three instances. In both John 1 and John 21 some of the ancient Greek manuscripts read *Iōna* (Jonah), apparently because of the attraction of the more familiar Simon Bar-Jona (Matt 16:17).

[59]In the Greek text, there are differences in the wording of the three questions. These differences are really insignificant from a theological point of view. From a merely literary point of view, they prevent the dialogue from becoming monotonous.

[60]John 18:18 and 21:9 are the only two places in the New Testament where mention is made of a charcoal fire *(anthrakia)*.

his question yet a third time, it is an upset Peter who replies, "Lord, you know everything; you know that I love you" (John 21:17). The additional reference to Jesus' knowledge contributes to the drama of the narration.

Scholars are generally convinced that Jesus' thrice repeated command to Peter, "feed my lambs . . . tend my sheep . . . feed my sheep," includes both a mandate of leadership within the Church of Jerusalem and a mandate to preach the Gospel.[61] The evangelist has previously indicated that Peter exercised the function of spokesperson for the group of the Twelve (John 6:67-69). In the epilogue's description of the encounter between the Risen Jesus and his disciples, Simon Peter is portrayed as acting in the name of the group of disciples (John 21:11). The account continues clearly to be post-resurrectional as the evangelist describes, in John 21:15-19, a role of ecclesial leadership being conferred upon Peter.[62]

That there exist two levels on which the Fourth Gospel is to be read makes it sometimes difficult for a reader to distinguish between those elements of the narrative that reflect the situation of the evangelist's community and those that reflect a more ancient tradition, perhaps reaching all the way back to Jesus' own lifetime. When, however, the Fourth Gospel portrays Simon Peter as exercising a leadership position among Jesus' disciples prior to his death and then describes a primacy being conferred upon Peter in the post-resurrectional era, the Gospel is reflecting the two-step foundation of the Church, of which the Gospel of Matthew also gives evidence.

Matthew's rendition of the conferral of primacy upon Peter is incorporated as an editorial insertion into his version of the story of Peter's confession in the area of Caesarea Philippi (Matt 16:13-20). Verses 13-16 and 20 of the Matthean narrative essentially reflect an older tradition on Peter's dominant position

---

[61]See, for example, Raymond E. Brown, *The Gospel According to John. XIII-XXI* (AB, 29A; Garden City, N.Y.: Doubleday, 1970) 1112-17, and R. E. Brown, K. P. Donfried, J. Reumann, eds., *Peter in the New Testament* (Minneapolis: Augsburg, 1973) 141-44.

[62]This is the evangelist's way of dealing with the common early Christian tradition of the special relationship between the resurrected Jesus and Peter. Cf. Luke 24:12; 1 Corinthians 15:5; Matthew 16:(16)17-19.

among Jesus' early disciples, as a comparison with the parallel accounts in Mark (Mark 8:27-30) and Luke (Luke 9:18-21) readily shows. However, verses 17-19 of the Matthean story essentially reflect a Matthean redaction of a post-resurrectional tradition. The older tradition points to Peter's position of prominence among the disciples of Jesus the itinerant preacher, while the redactional insertion points to the position of primacy that Peter enjoyed within the Church as a result of his confession of the Risen One.

The fourth evangelist has his own way of portraying these two distinctive modes of Peter's leadership among the disciples. He uses his own categories and the symbols familiar to his community. Nonetheless, the evangelist attests to both the ancient tradition of the role played by Peter among the disciples during Jesus' public ministry and Peter's primatial role among those disciples because of his personal encounter of the Risen One.

Simon Peter

If the fourth evangelist acknowledges Peter's traditional role among the first disciples of Jesus while nonetheless portraying it in his own words, he has chosen to use the figure of Peter to portray what was, from the evangelist's own perspective, the ambiguity inherent in the faith of those early disciples. The Peter who was the spokesperson for the Twelve comes to the fore as the symbolic expression of that ambiguity. Peter's faith pales in comparison with that of the beloved disciple.

The evangelist's less-than-laudatory portrayal of the situation of the Twelve and the complexity of his portrayal of Simon Peter serve as signs of the relative independence of the evangelist's community vis-à-vis the apostolic Churches. Whereas Simon Peter symbolizes the ambiguity of their faith, the beloved disciple symbolizes the purity of faith of the evangelist's own community. While the apostolic Churches adhered to the tradition of Peter's leadership among the Twelve and to his post-resurrectional faith, the evangelist's community found their distinctive foundational support in the faith witness of the beloved disciple. Their relative independence from the apostolic communities gave them an almost sectarian status among the Christian communities of the late first century.

The epilogue (John 21) was added to the Gospel by a hand other than that of the evangelist.[63] Nevertheless, he belonged to the same circles as the evangelist and imitated his style. In his epilogue, the figure of Peter appears in a new light. To be sure, the pairing of Peter with the beloved disciple is characteristic of the evangelist's community's way of looking at Peter. So, too, is the recognition that he must first of all be considered as a disciple. Nonetheless, as a result of the primacy interview Simon Peter, who has been shown to be a man of resurrectional faith, is portrayed as a man of love and is entrusted with pastoral responsibility for Jesus' own, his lambs and his sheep.[64]

The entire scene represents the rehabilitation of the figure of Peter within the evangelist's own circles. They accept the primatial role accorded to Peter within the apostolic communities, all the while expecting that those communities would acknowledge the continuing vitality of the testimony of the beloved disciple.[65]

---

[63]My conviction that John 21 was added to an earlier version of the Gospel by a different hand in no way implies my endorsement of Rudolf Bultmann's views on the "ecclesiastical redactor." See R. Bultmann, *The Gospel of John,* an English language translation of a classic which originally appeared in German in 1940. Bultmann envisioned the work of this redactor as not only adding chapter 21 to the Gospel, but also as otherwise reworking the text so as to make it acceptable as a document of "early catholicism."

[64]Cf. John 10:1-18.

[65]Cf. John 21:21-22.

5

Philip

The story of Philip's encounter with Jesus (John 1:43-46) seems to represent a new beginning in the evangelist's story. Not only is Philip the only disciple to be called in classic fashion—called, that is, to "follow me" (John 1:43)—but the evangelist has also placed the time of the encounter on a new day. A by now familiar "the next day"[1] separates the evangelist's introduction of Philip from his initial presentation of Simon Peter (John 1:41-42). Jesus is presented as being in a decisive mood:[2] he has made the decision to go into Galilee.[3] Galilee is home turf for the named disciples—Andrew, Simon Peter, Philip, and Nathanael all come from Galilee. Having made his decision, Jesus seeks out and finds Philip. Then Jesus addresses the call to Philip: "Follow me."

Jesus' initiative in the call of Philip and the classic formulation of his invitation distinguish the evangelist's account of Philip's call from his previous descriptions of discipleship. Andrew had found Simon Peter and brought him to Jesus, but it is Jesus who finds Philip and addresses an explicit invitation to Philip to follow him. Although the manner of Philip's call is unusual—at least from the perspective of the fourth evangelist's narrative—the result of his acceptance of the call to discipleship

---

[1]Cf. John 1:29, 35.

[2]The verb "to decide" *(thelō)* is rarely used of Jesus in the Fourth Gospel. Cf. John 5:21; 7:1 (closely parallel with 1:44); 17:24; 21:22, 23.

[3]Cf. John 4:3, 43, 45, 46, 47, 54. Other Fourth Gospel references to Galilee are in John 2:1, 11; 6:1; 7:1, 9, 41, 52 (twice); 12:21; 21:2.

is typical. Philip becomes a Christian herald. He seeks out a fellow Galilean, Nathanael, and announces, "We have found him of whom Moses in the law and also the prophets wrote, Jesus of Nazareth, the son of Joseph" (John 1:45).

The new disciple's profession of faith is striking. He has made a profound Christological statement: He has identified Jesus of Nazareth,[4] the son of Joseph, as the one to whom the Scriptures bear witness. The precise significance of the Christological statement need not detain us here, but one might take note of the unusual phrase "of whom Moses in the law and also the prophets wrote." A reader generally familiar with the New Testament might have expected the evangelist to write about "the law and the prophets,"[5] but that is not what he has written.

The phraseology is the evangelist's very own, and it is typical of his work. The verb is in the singular with the phrase "and the prophets" appearing as an add-on.[6] The unusual turn of phrase might indicate that rather than suggest that the generality of the Jewish Scriptures testify to Jesus,[7] the evangelist has a particular text or tradition in mind. If so, the Scripture to which the evangelist's Philip alludes might well be Deuteronomy 18:18[8] with its reference to the prophet similar to Moses.[9]

Philip is obviously a disciple—he even offers an invitation to discipleship similar to that of Jesus himself[10]—but his name is not included in the list of disciples cited in the epilogue to the

[4]This is the only time in the Fourth Gospel that Jesus is called "Jesus of Nazareth." See, further, John 1:46.

[5]See Matthew 5:17; 7:12; 11:13; 22:40; Luke 16:16; 24:44, Acts 13:15; 24:14.

[6]Literally, therefore, ". . . him of whom Moses in the law wrote and also the prophets." For an earlier example of the evangelist's use of a verb in the singular to which an add-on has been appended, see John 1:36.

[7]Cf. John 5:39.

[8]This interpretation has been forcefully argued by M.-E. Boismard in *Moïse ou Jésus: Essai de christologie johannique* (Bibliotheca Ephemeridum Theologicarum Lovaniensium, 84; Louvain: University Press, 1988) 29–33. Boismard also interprets the expression "son of Joseph" as a double entendre (see pp. 33–41). Not only would it identify Jesus as the son of Joseph the carpenter, it would also allude to Joseph, the patriarch, who played a role in Samaritan speculations, where he was sometimes portrayed as a royal figure.

[9]Cf. John 1:21.

[10]Cf. John 1:39 and John 1:46.

Gospel (John 21:2). Each of the Synoptists lists Philip among the
Twelve,[11] but the fourth evangelist does not identify Philip as one
of the Twelve. Nothing else is said about Philip in the Synoptics,
but more indeed is said about him in the Fourth Gospel.

In the Synoptic Gospels Philip appears only as a name. In the
Fourth Gospel he appears as a real character. After the evangelist's
introduction of Philip as a disciple of Jesus (John 1:43-46), Philip
appears in three other scenes, John 6:1-15; 12:20-36; and 14:1-14.
What role does Philip have to play in the story? How does the
fourth evangelist characterize him? Whom or what does he represent?

John 6:5-7

Paired with Andrew, Philip appears in the story of the feeding
of the five thousand.[12] As was the case in the evangelist's narrative of Philip's call, it is Jesus who takes the initiative in the encounter with Philip. He asks Philip a simple question, "How are
we to buy bread, so that these people may eat?" (John 6:5). In
a typical Johannine aside (v. 6), the evangelist explains that Jesus'
question was not quite innocent. The question was phrased as a
test for Philip, because Jesus himself knew what he was about
to do.[13]

It is not unusual for the evangelist to highlight the superhuman knowledge of Jesus and to use the characters of his story
as foils in order to accentuate the special nature of Jesus' knowledge.[14] Yet there may be more to this story than merely that. The
evangelist clearly interprets the tradition of Jesus' feeding the
crowds in the light of the biblical tradition of Yahweh providing
manna for his people to eat at the time of the Exodus.[15] The Book

---

[11]Matthew 10:3; Mark 3:19; Luke 6:14. In all three instances the name of Philip is paired
with that of Bartholomew.

[12]He does not appear in the Synoptic accounts of this miracle. See ch. 3 above, pp. 62–63.

[13]The Johannine tradition may well have been influenced by Genesis 22:1-14 at this point.
See C. T. Ruddick, Jr., "Feeding and Sacrifice—the Old Testament Background of the Fourth
Gospel," *Expository Times* 79 (1968) 340–41.

[14]See John 1:48, 50 and 4:17-18 as examples of this technique.

[15]See, especially, John 6:25-40.

of Deuteronomy interprets the various Exodus events as signs and as tests.[16] In similar fashion, the evangelist, for whom the feeding is manifestly a sign *(sēmeion,* John 6:26, 30), here proclaims that is is a test as well.

Philip fails his test. He does not understand that Jesus will make provision for the people. He projects the figure of a human being who cannot understand the action of God. As such, Philip represents the misunderstanding of the disciples. Previously (John 4:31-38) the evangelist had portrayed the group of Jesus' disciples as a group prone to misunderstanding. Their misunderstanding was revealed in their failure to comprehend the nature of Jesus' "food." Now Philip is singled out as a disciple who misunderstands. His misunderstanding is revealed in his failure to understand Jesus' ability to provide food for the people.[17] He represents the misunderstanding disciple, just as Thomas will later represent the disciple who doubts.

Misunderstanding is a major device used in the composition of the Fourth Gospel,[18] which the evangelist employs in a variety of ways. He uses it to show that the world remains in the state of unbelief. He also uses it to show that even a disciple can fail in understanding when confronted by divine action. Philip had shown himself to be a real disciple by bringing Nathanael to Jesus, but he fails the test of discipleship when Jesus is about to provide bread for his people.

John 12:20-22

Philip next appears in the Fourth Gospel on the occasion of a feast (John 12:20-36). Once again he is making a Passover ap-

---

[16]See Deuteronomy 4:34; 7:19; 29:2; comp. 8:16; 13:4. Cf. Donatien Mollat, *Etudes johanniques* (Parole de Dieu, 3; Paris: Seuil, 1979) 98.

[17]Cf. Mark 6:52; comp. Mark 8:16-21; Matthew 16:7-12.

[18]Cf. Herbert Leroy, *Rätsel und Missverständnis: Ein Beitrag zur Formgeschichte des Johannesevangeliums* (Bonner biblische Beiträge, 30; Bonn: Hanstein, 1968); Donald A. Carson, "Understanding Misunderstandings in the Fourth Gospel," *Tyndale Bulletin* 33 (1982) 59–91; and R. Alan Culpepper, *Anatomy of the Fourth Gospel: A Study in Literary Design* (New Testament Foundations and Facets; Philadelphia: Fortress, 1983) 152–165.

pearance.[19] The evangelist introduces some Greeks and Andrew into the scene along with Philip (vv. 20-21), but the real principals are Jesus and the disciples,[20] to whom the ensuing discourse (vv. 22-36) is directed. The evangelist uses Andrew and Philip to make his discourse concrete. Their presence adds realism and dramatic flair to the narrative.

Philip is approached by some Greeks who want to see Jesus. It may not be incidental that Philip hails from Bethsaida, a town the evangelist locates in Galilee.[21] Galilee, situated on the frontiers of Israel, was well known as the land of the Gentiles.[22] Philip had a Greek name, one borne by a Macedonian king long centuries before. Thus, at the Fourth Gospel's narrative level, these Greeks can expect to find in Philip a sympathetic ear and a willing intermediary. Nonetheless, the evangelist's other concerns are apparent. As the Samaritans were introduced to Jesus by the testimony of a Samaritan woman (John 4:28), the Greeks are introduced to Jesus by one who represents the Greek disciples.[23]

Though qualified for the task of introducing the Greeks to Jesus, Philip appeals to Andrew. For the second time in the Fourth Gospel Philip is paired with Andrew.[24] Compared with Simon Peter's brother, Philip appears to be less perceptive, less sure of his relationship with Jesus. Archbishop Bernard calls him "cautious, perhaps a little dull!"[25] Only accompanied by Andrew does Philip go to tell Jesus about the Greeks who want to see him.

---

[19]After Philip's initial call to discipleship, each of his appearances is a Passover appearance. See John 6:4; 12:20 (cf. 12:1); and, for the discourse during the farewell meal, John 13:1.

[20]See Godfrey C. Nicholson, *Death as Departure: The Johannine Descent-Ascent Schema* (Society of Biblical Literature Dissertation Series, 63; Chico, Calif.: Scholars, 1983) 124.

[21]See ch. 3 above, n. 12.

[22]See, for example, the citation of Isaiah 9:1 in Matthew 4:15.

[23]Andrew is also a Greek, rather than a Semitic, name.

[24]See John 6:5-7.

[25]See J. H. Bernard, *A Critical and Exegetical Commentary on the Gospel According to St. John* (International Critical Commentary; Edinburgh: Clark, 1928) 431.

John 14:8-11

Philip's lack of perception comes most clearly to the fore on the occasion of Jesus' farewell meal,[26] a scene in which Philip makes his final appearance (John 14:8-14) as he assumes a representative function. He speaks on behalf of the disciples when he says, "Lord, show us the Father, and we shall be satisfied" (John 14:8). Philip's use of the pronoun in the first person plural *(hēmin,* twice) is a clear expression of the role he has assumed. In the ensuing discourse, Jesus responds in the second person plural (John 14:10b-14). He speaks to the disciples as a group.

Jesus' address to the disciples is, however, preceded by a rebuke directed to Philip. Jesus speaks in the second person singular (John 14:9-10a).[27] That Philip is singled out from the other disciples is readily apparent in the initial rebuke: "Have I been with *you* so long, and yet *you* do not *know* me, Philip?" (John 14:9a). The contrast between the pronoun in the plural *(humin,* "you") and the verb in the singular *(egnōkas,* "you know"), followed by "Philip" *(Philippe),* a vocative emphatically placed at the end of the sentence, accentuates the sharpness of Jesus' rebuke. It is directed to Philip and to him alone.

Why does Philip merit such a rebuke and a dressing-down (vv. 9b-10a) by Jesus? Because he has expected a theophany. He has expected that the disciples would be graced with an appearance of the God of Israel such as Moses, Aaron, and the elders of Israel had experienced.[28] No such an appearance is to be had. Sufficient for those who truly believe is the experience of Jesus and the acceptance of his revelatory words.

Ironically, Philip, who wants to see,[29] has not seen. He appears as one who has not truly seen Jesus, for "he who has seen me

---

[26]Apropos its connection with the Passover, see John 13:1.

[27]In Greek, the difference between the singular and plural number of the pronouns and the verbs is readily apparent. It is not so apparent in English, where "you" functions as both a singular and a plural pronoun, and whose verb forms distinguish only verbs used in the third person singular.

[28]Exodus 24:9-10.

[29]Cf. John 12:21, where Philip is asked to serve as intermediary for the group of Greeks who want to *see Jesus (ton Iēsoun idein).*

has seen the Father" (v. 9b). Philip has not enjoyed the insight
that comes with faith. Hence Jesus examines Philip about the quality of his faith: "Do you not believe that I am in the Father and
the Father in me?" The negative question normally demands a
positive response, but no response from Philip is forthcoming,
according to the evangelist's account. Instead, he continues his
story with Jesus' instruction to his disciples on the significance
of faith and the nature of his own relationship with the Father.

At this point the figure of Philip disappears from the fourth
evangelist's narrative. His discipleship started out so well. Called
by Jesus, he used biblical categories to identify Jesus for the benefit of Nathanael. He brought Nathanael to Jesus. In this respect,
his discipleship is complete. But then he fails the bread test. He
even fails his Greek test.[30] At the end, he seems to fail the real
test of discipleship because he fails to see Jesus.[31] Perhaps, then,
it is not really so surprising that the name of Philip is omitted
from the epilogue's list of the disciples of Jesus (John 21:2).

[30]See Culpepper, *Anatomy,* 120.
[31]Cf. 1:39, 46.

6

Nathanael

In contrast with Philip, whose name does not appear on the list of disciples appended to the Fourth Gospel at John 21:2, the name of Nathanael does appear—virtually in bold print. He is solemnly identified as "Nathanael of Cana in Galilee." He has been previously introduced to Jesus—and, incidentally, to the reader of the Gospel—by Philip. "Philip found Nathanael, and said to him, 'We have found him of whom Moses in the law and also the prophets wrote, Jesus of Nazareth, the son of Joseph' " (John 1:45).

Nathanael is someone whose name does not appear at all in the Synoptic Gospels. Unlike Andrew, Simon Peter, and Philip, disciples whose names at least appear in those Gospels, and unlike John, the witness whose figure appears in the Synoptics albeit with a different configuration, Nathanael does not appear in any New Testament book except the Gospel of John.

A harmonized reading of the various New Testament accounts, so characteristic of a popular and "more traditional" interpretation, tended to identify Nathanael with the Bartholomew of the Synoptic Gospels.[1] The portal of the Latin rite Church in Kefar Kanna (the village of Cana, Israel) even bears witness to this confusion. Yet there is not a shred of historical evidence that Nathanael and Bartholomew were the same person. The most plausible reason for the traditional confusion of the two is that

---

[1]The identification of Nathanael and Bartholomew was also supported by some of the earlier critics, such as Ernest Renan and Theodor Zahn.

"the disciples" were often identified with "the twelve apostles." Since Nathanael is clearly portrayed as a disciple in the Fourth Gospel, his name somehow *must* have appeared among the Twelve. In the Synoptics' listings of the Twelve, the name of Bartholomew comes after that of Philip.[2] In addition, Bartholomew is a patronymic name,[3] thus leaving open the possibility that the gentleman had another name, his given name. These factors facilitated the identification of Nathanael with Bartholomew, which confusion was virtually required by a somewhat naive understanding of discipleship.[4]

"What's in a name?"[5] The theophoric Hebrew name Nathanael[6] means "God has given" and is equivalent to the Greek name Theodore. However, it is not upon the name Nathanael that the evangelist dwells as he narrates the story in John 1:45-51. His focus is upon Jesus' words, the climax of which is in the solemn revelatory statement of verse 51: "Truly, truly, I say to you, you will see heaven opened, and the angels of God ascending and descending upon the Son of man."

Before Jesus' dialogue with Nathanael reaches its climax in this utterance, Jesus had proved himself to be a revealer and someone gifted with superhuman knowledge. The Christological aspects of this passage need not detain us here. For our purposes it is significant that the evangelist uses the revelatory formula[7] as he writes of Jesus saying to Nathanael, "Behold, an Israelite indeed, in whom is no guile" (John 1:47). Nathanael is the only figure in any of the four Gospels who merits to be called an "Israelite."

---

[2]See Matthew 10:3; Mark 3:18; Luke 6:14; Acts 1:13.

[3]See ch. 4 above, n. 12.

[4]Raymond Brown suggests that since there was no standard list of names for the Twelve, the Johannine community might have had a list of the Twelve different from those available to the Synoptic authors. See R. E. Brown, *The Community of the Beloved Disciple* (New York: Paulist, 1979) 81, n. 149. In which case Nathanael might have been known to the community as one of the Twelve. In any case, he is not so identified within the Fourth Gospel.

[5]*Romeo and Juliet,* II, 2.

[6]See Numbers 1:8. Moreover, a man named Simeon ben Nathanael was a second generation Tannaitic rabbi (ca. A.D. 80–120).

[7]See above, p. 28.

What is the meaning of this name, whose enigmatic character is hinted at by dint of its appearance in the revelation formula?

A provocative question

Philip has faithfully responded to his own call to discipleship by bringing Nathanael to Jesus. He has identified Jesus as the one "of whom Moses in the law and also the prophets wrote" (John 1:45).[8] This testimony is not immediately convincing to Nathanael. It is enough to convince Nathanael that Philip is claiming some sort of messianic status for Jesus, but it is not enough to convince Nathanael of the validity of that claim. He immediately objects, "Can anything good come out of Nazareth?"

This objection, centering as it does on Jesus' origins, belongs to a body of tradition, to which the Fourth Gospel bears witness on several occasions, that Jesus' status has been called into question because of his origins. The issue is brought to the surface in John 7:40-43. That discussion proves to be inconclusive, even though it is enough to establish that the royal Messiah ought not to have Galilean origins. So an appeal is made to the authorities, represented by Nicodemus.[9] That discussion results in a scripturally based affirmation that no prophet is to come from Galilee.[10] Thus, according to the Scriptures, apparently narrowly interpreted, neither the Messiah nor the prophet[11] is to be a Galilean.

In the eyes of the evangelist, however, Jesus' messianic status is not based on his Davidic origins; neither is it based on his superhuman powers. Rather, it is based on Jesus' origin from God.[12] Nonetheless, the evangelist is well aware that scripturally based arguments had been contrived in order to deny Jesus' true identification. Perhaps his Nathanael is one of those who had, with

---

[8]This testimony is interpreted as a call *(phōneō)* in John 1:48.

[9]Cf. John 7:50; 3:1.

[10]Cf. John 7:52.

[11]Cf. John 1:20.

[12]See Peter Pokorny, "Der irdische Jesus im Johannesevangelium" *New Testament Studies* 30 (1984) 217–228, p. 223.

the prophet Micah,[13] expected the Messiah to come from some place other than the obscure Galilean town of Nazareth.[14] In any event, it is Philip's identification of Jesus as Jesus *of Nazareth* that initially proves problematic for an incredulous Nathanael. Thus, the question, "Can anything good come out of Nazareth?"

Philip's response, "Come and see," recalls the words that Jesus addressed to the first pair of disciples (John 1:39). The words are an invitation to discipleship, addressed to one who is nonetheless hesitant. Apparently Nathanael responds positively to the invitation because he is approaching Jesus when "Jesus saw Nathanael coming to him, and said of him, 'Behold, an Israelite indeed, in whom is no guile' " (John 1:47).

At this point, the evangelist's portrayal of discipleship remains consistent. Nathanael is called to discipleship by the testimony of someone else, Philip. The object of discipleship is seeing Jesus, that is, seeing Jesus with the insight that comes from belief in him. Nathanael goes to Jesus as did the first two disciples and Peter. Discipleship embodies a personal relationship with Jesus, in this case suggested by the image of Jesus' perception of Nathanael and the enigmatic epithet with which Nathanael is addressed.

A hesitant Nathanael responds with yet another expression of incredulity, "How did you know me?" (John 1:48). Jesus' own response to this question, "Before Philip called you, when you were under the fig tree, I saw you" (John 1:48b), is an expression of his superhuman knowledge, a Christological motif dear to the evangelist and his community.[15] Ironically, Nathanael, who comes with Philip to see Jesus, has been seen by Jesus even before his encounter with Philip. Indeed, Nathanael has been twice seen by Jesus, once while he was on the way to Jesus, and once prior to his being found by Philip. He is a person who has been seen by Jesus both before and after he receives Philip's testimony.

It may well be that the evangelist, whose careful attention to places is present throughout his entire work, is not innocent in

[13]See Micah 5:1.

[14]The town of Nazareth is not mentioned even once in the Old Testament.

[15]Cf. John 2:25; 4:17-18; 6:6; etc.

placing Nathanael under the fig tree[16] at the moment that he is first seen by Jesus. Rabbinic literature often depicts rabbis discussing the Torah with their disciples while sitting under a fig tree.[17] Thus the evangelist may well be subtly suggesting that the Nathanael who comes to Jesus is indeed a student of the Law. In any event, Nathanael proclaims Jesus to be a teacher of the Law. He calls him rabbi: "Rabbi, you are the Son of God! You are the king of Israel!"(John 1:49).

A Confession of Faith

The response is, in fact, a response to Jesus' superhuman knowledge. Nathanael is a man who comes to faith as a result of the manifestation of the superhuman powers that lie within Jesus.[18] In this respect, Nathanael's faith in Jesus is similar to that of those who believe in Jesus because of the signs he has done.[19] A veritable litany flows from his lips as he confesses Jesus to be rabbi, Son of God, and king of Israel. It is a full confession of faith, summing up the progression from a relatively low confession of Christological faith, symbolized by the title "Rabbi," to a relatively high confession of Christological faith, symbolized by the "Son of God" and "King of Israel" titles, in a single catena. Each of these titles represents an epitome of traditional Jewish messianic expectations, the "Son of God" recalling such biblical passages as 2 Samuel 7:14 and Psalm 2:7 and "King of Israel" serving as a common messianic title in late Judaism.[20]

---

[16]This is a significant motif in iconography. See Rainer Stichel, *Nathanael unter dem Feigenbaum: Die Geschichte eines biblischen Erzahlstoffes in Literatur und Kunst der byzantinischen Welt* (Stuttgart: Steiner, 1985).

[17]See Hermann L. Strack—Paul Billerbeck, *Kommentar zum Neuen Testament aus Talmud und Midrasch,* vol. 2: *Das Evangelium nach Markus, Lukas und Johannes und die Apostelgeschichte* (Munich: Beck, 1924) 371; Siegfried Schulz, *Das Evangelium nach Johannes,* 42; F. Hahn, "Die Jungerberufung Joh. 1, 35–51," in J. Gnilka, ed., *Neues Testament und Kirche* (Fs. R. Schnackenburg; Freiburg: Herder, 1974) 172–190, pp. 187–188.

[18]In the history of the tradition behind the Fourth Gospel, it may be that the "Son of God" title is a specific response to Jesus' manifestation of superhuman knowledge.

[19]See John 20:30–31.

[20]See John 12:13. Cf. John 6:15; Matthew 27:37; Mark 15:26; Luke 23:38; John 19:19.

Only one other person in the Fourth Gospel, Martha, professes belief in Jesus by proclaiming him to be Son of God. In response to Jesus' question about her belief, she solemnly avows, "Yes, Lord; I believe that you are the Christ, the Son of God, he who is coming into the world" (John 11:27). The cumulation of Christological titles that Martha uses in an attempt to express the fullness of her faith response recalls the catena of Christological titles that flow from Nathanael's lips.

In Nathanael's case, the emphasis clearly lies upon his confession of Jesus as king of Israel.[21] The identification of the Messiah had been in the air during the four days of meetings and discussion described by the evangelist in John 1:19-49. "King of Israel" is in the final, climactic position in the short litany of Christological titles that flow from Nathanael's lips. It recalls the enigmatic epithet with which Jesus addressed Nathanael when he called him "an Israelite indeed." Jesus' subsequent response to Nathanael's confession recalls the vision of Jacob-Israel at Bethel.[22]

That the evangelist suggests that Nathanael is a person familiar with the Scriptures cannot be overlooked. Philip has presented Jesus to him as someone to whom the Scriptures testify. Nathanael has an objection, apparently based on those same Scriptures. He is seen by Jesus while sitting under the fig tree, a typical locale for a rabbinic searching of the Scriptures. Nathanael calls Jesus "Rabbi." Finally, Jesus promises him[23] a vision, which is described in terms of Genesis 28:12. The entire scenario breathes the air of the intepretation of the Scriptures.

Nathanael's confession of faith in Jesus is the climax of the entire discussion on messiahship that began when the official delegation asked John "Who are you" and John responded "I am not the Christ" (John 1:19-20).[24] Jesus responded to Nathanael's

---

[21]Schulz even suggests that "Son of God" might be a later addition by the evangelist. See *Das Evangelium nach Johannes,* 42.

[22]See John 1:51; Genesis 28:12.

[23]And the community. Note the plural "you will see" *(opsesthe)* in v. 51.

[24]See Francis J. Moloney, *The Johannine Son of Man* (Biblioteca di Scienze religiose, 14; Rome: LAS, 1976) 35.

messianic confession with a question, "Do you believe because
I said to you, I saw you under the fig tree?" (John 1:50a) and
a promise.

In the evangelist's narrative Jesus does not allow Nathanael the
opportunity to answer the question about the quality of his faith.
Instead, the reprise of the theme of verse 48, Nathanael under
the fig tree, allows the Jesus who has taken the initiative throughout this pericope (vv. 43-44) to go further. Expecting a positive
response to his question, he promises "You shall see greater things
than these" (John 1:50b).

The Promise of a Vision

Immediately thereafter Jesus tells Nathanael about the nature
of the vision of the greater things that he is to enjoy: "Truly, truly,
I say to you, you will see heaven opened, and the angels of God
ascending and descending upon the Son of man" (John 1:51).[25]
This expression of Jesus' self-revelation is the real climax of the
narrative that began in John 1:19, and it serves as a magnificent
reminder that discipleship is fulfilled in the vision of Jesus (see
John 1:39). While the statement is ostensibly addressed to
Nathanael,[26] it is really addressed to all disciples. Jesus' words
are in the plural: "Truly, truly, I say to you [the plural *humin*],
you will see [the plural *opsesthe*] heaven opened."[27] The words
are really addressed to the believers of the evangelist's own community who have come to know that they will see Jesus as the
Son of Man.[28]

---

[25]"Man" is the traditional translation of the Greek gender neutral *anthrōpos*. Some scholars accordingly prefer to translate *anthrōpos* by some other term, e.g., humanity. In this
as in many other respects, the discussion of the exact meaning of *ho huios tou anthrōpou*
(Son of man) is far too technical to be entered upon in a book of the length and purpose
of the present work.

[26]"And he said *to him (auto)*. . . ."

[27]The plural form of the verb leads most commentators to the conviction that in the history
of the tradition, John 1:51 was originally an independent saying which the evangelist has
added to the narrative at this point.

[28]See John 1:51; 3:13, 14; 5:27; 6:27, 53, 62; 8:28; 9:35; 12:23, 34 (twice); 13:31; and
Moloney's aforementioned study, *The Johannine Son of Man*.

That Jesus responds to Nathanael's solemn messianic confession of faith with a statement about the Son of Man comes as no surprise to readers familiar with the New Testament's fourfold Gospel tradition. In the Synoptic Gospels, Jesus responds to Peter's messianic confession of faith with a statement about the fate of the Son of Man.[29] In the Fourth Gospel, Jesus' confession-response does not focus upon his suffering and death as it does in the Synoptics; rather, it focuses upon a vision to be enjoyed by those who believe in him.

Jesus' words recall the dream of Jacob-Israel at Bethel. "He dreamed that there was a ladder set up on the earth, and the top of it reached to heaven; and behold, the angels of God were ascending and descending on it!" (Gen 28:12). Late Jewish speculation about the stone at Bethel (literally, the "house of God") frequently focused on it as the place of God's presence or the place over which is to be found the gateway to heaven. The recollection of such speculation provides an entree for the use of Genesis 28:12 in John 1:51.

The evangelist quotes the biblical text rather exactly, that is, until he comes to the end of the verse. There he substitutes "on the Son of man" for the traditional "on it" *(ep'autēs,* that is, the ladder). Thus, the use of the text of Genesis 28:12 seems to be an accommodated use or a bit of paraphrase. In fact, the evangelist seems to be familiar with the Jewish practice of paraphrasing biblical texts in order to accommodate them to contemporary situations. It is in this fashion that he uses Genesis 18:17 (Abraham's laughter) in John 8:56, and Isaiah 6:10 (Isaiah's vision) in John 12:41.

The Jewish tradition of paraphrasing their Scriptures led to the formation of the various targums.[30] The extant Aramaic targums, whose exact dating is difficult to determine, help to clarify the meaning of Genesis 28:12 as it is used by the evangelist in John

---

[29]Mark 8:29, 31; Luke 9:20, 22; cf. Matthew 16:16, 21.

[30]Principally the Targum Onkelos, the Targum of Pseudo-Jonathan, Targum Neofiti I, and the so-called Fragment Targum. An English-language edition of the Targums, *The Aramaic Bible,* is being published by The Liturgical Press.

1:51.[31] As a representative of the fourth evangelist's faith community, Nathanael is promised a vision of angels ascending and descending upon the Son of Man.

As he writes of Nathanael, the evangelist's thought is moving in the world of Jewish apocalyptic. The opened heavens are a classic apocalyptic motif. Sometimes the heavens are opened so that someone or something can descend to earth;[32] sometimes the heavens are opened so that a seer can experience a vision of heavenly realities.[33]

The evangelist shares the Jewish conviction[34] that no one can see God (John 1:18; 5:37; 6:46). Like the author of 4 Ezra,[35] more or less contemporary with himself, the author of the Fourth Gospel takes issue[36] with those who claim that one or another privileged visionary has entered heaven, thereby being qualified to return to earth in order to reveal divine secrets. In the evangelist's vision of things it is Jesus alone who enjoys that kind of intimacy with God.[37]

How then does the evangelist deal with the tradition of the biblical theophanies? A case in point is the famous vision in which the prophet Isaiah saw the glory of the Lord (Isa 6). The evangelist interprets the tradition in such a way as to affirm that it was really Jesus who had been seen by Isaiah (John 12:41) just as he has earlier indicated that Abraham had seen not a theophany but the day of Jesus.[38] In this respect the evangelist's mode of dealing with the tradition of the theophanies enjoyed by the bib-

---

[31]See, especially, Jerome H. Neyrey, "The Jacob Allusions in John 1:51," *Catholic Biblical Quarterly* 44 (1982) 586–605 and C. C. Rowland, "John 1:51, Jewish Apocalyptic and Targumic Tradition," *New Testament Studies* 30 (1984) 498–507.

[32]See such passages as Isaiah 64:1; 3 Maccabees 6:18; Matthew 3:16; Mark 1:10; Acts 10:11.

[33]See, for example, Ezekiel 1:1; Acts 7:56; Revelation 11:19; 14:5; 19:11. Cf. Revelation 4:1.

[34]See Exodus 33:20-23; Deuteronomy 4:12. Cf. Philo, *De Specialibus Legibus,* I, VIII, 41-50.

[35]See 4 Ezra 4:8; 8:21.

[36]See John 3:13.

[37]See John 3:13; 6:46. Cf. John 1:18.

[38]See John 8:56.

lical heroes is akin to that of Philo, who wrote that Moses saw not the glory of God but his powers.[39]

What then is the nature of the promise made to the believers represented by Nathanael? That they would experience a theophany. Not of God himself, to be sure, but of the Son of Man in his glory.[40] The ascending and descending angels represent so many heavenly courtiers approaching the throne of the Son of Man and coming away from the throne. What Jesus promises the believers is a Christophany, that is, a vision of himself in glory. In fact, that is the most that believers can really hope for. From the perspective that reigned in the evangelist's circle, it is impossible to see God.[41] But there is really no need for the believer to see God, for the one who truly sees Jesus has seen the Father.[42]

Apparently the evangelist has accepted the popular etymology of the name of Israel, that is, "one who sees God."[43] According to the biblical tradition, Jacob received this new name precisely because he had experienced a theophany. He was one who had seen God. Nathanael was not to enjoy a theophany. Nonetheless, the seeing motif permeates the scene in which he appears.[44] In the end Nathanael will prove to be "an Israelite indeed," that is, one who truly sees God. He will enjoy the vision of the manifestation of God, the Son of Man upon whom the angels of God ascend and descend.

The Nathanael of the Fourth Gospel is a disciple who sees. As the true Israelite, he stands in contrast with "the Jews." Their messianic investigation brings them to John but not—at least at this point in the Gospel narrative—to Jesus. They search the Scriptures but object to Jesus' messiahship on the basis of those same Scriptures (John 7:27, 41-42, 52) and refuse to come to Jesus (John

---

[39]Philo, *De Specialibus Legibus*, I, VIII, 46. Cf. J. Neyrey, *art. cit.*, 592.

[40]Cf. John 14:8-9.

[41]See John 1:18.

[42]See John 14:9.

[43]See Genesis 32:28-30.

[44]" 'Come and *see*.' . . . Jesus *saw* Nathanael. . . . '*Behold*, . . . I *saw* you. . . . I *saw* you. . . . You *shall see* greater things . . . you *will see* heaven opened . . . ' " (John 1:46-51).

5:39-40). Their father is the devil in whom there is no truth (John 8:44). They ask the question "Who are you?" (John 8:25) but do not understand what Jesus says (John 8:43).

Nathanael has no need to query "who are you?" He has received the testimony of Philip. He has heard the claim that Jesus fulfills the Scripture (John 1:45). A student of the Scriptures,[45] he has scrutinized the scriptural claims that have been made with regard to Jesus (John 1:46). Despite his difficulties, he goes to Jesus and addresses him as someone from whom he can learn the meaning of the Scriptures ("Rabbi," v. 49).[46] The vision that he is promised is one described in scriptural terms.[47] Nathanael, then, is typified as a guileless searcher of the Scriptures, one who has found what he was searching for. Thus he merits to be called "an Israelite indeed," a real Israelite.

In fact, while "the Jews" are generally portrayed in a negative fashion in the Fourth Gospel,[48] "Israel" is a term with positive connotations.[49] The evangelist seems to share with Paul a positive evaluation of "Israel,"[50] a meaningful quantity from the standpoint of salvation history. If Jacob-Israel is the type, Nathanael is the antitype. He is the "true Israelite."[51] In this capacity he represents the faithful Scripture-searching disciples of

---

[45]Note the symbolic localization of Nathanael under the fig tree (John 1:48, 50).

[46]Cf. John 3:2. One of the major themes of the Nicodemus discourse (John 3:1-15) is the contrast between Nicodemus, presumably well versed in the law, and Jesus, who is the true teacher capable of truly explicating the Scriptures. See R. F. Collins, "Jesus' Conversation with Nicodemus," *The Bible Today* 93 (1977) 1409-1418, in *These Things Have Been Written,* 56-67.

[47]Cf. the allusion to Genesis 28:12 in John 1:51.

[48]"The Jews" is an expression commonly used in the Fourth Gospel. Most frequently used with a pejorative connotation, it does not refer to the Jewish nation as such; rather, it refers to certain of its leaders (see ch. 1 above, p. 9). In the Fourth Gospel the Jews typify unbelief. See, further, Urban C. von Wahlde, "The Johannine 'Jews': A Critical Survey," *New Testament Studies* 28 (1982) 33-60.

[49]See John 1:31; 3:10; 12:13.

[50]Cf. Romans 9:4; 11:1; 2 Corinthians 11:22; Galatians 6:16.

[51]In Greek, *alēthōs Israelitēs.* Commentators have occasionally suggested that the root *alēth-* is frequently used in the Fourth Gospel with the connotation of a present reality in contrast to the past foreshadowing, for example, in the expression "true bread come down from heaven" (John 6:32) and "true vine" (John 15:1).

Jesus, who, in the evangelist's own times, were in conflict with "the Jews."[52]

Among these disciples there is nonetheless a subtle contrast between Nathanael and Philip. Philip proclaims to Nathanael that Jesus fulfills the Scriptures (John 1:45) and leads Nathanael to Jesus. Jesus proclaims Nathanael to be "truly an Israelite," that is, one who truly sees, and promises him a vision of the Son of Man in glory. In the end, however, Philip appears as one who has not truly seen Jesus (John 14:8-10). Nathanael is a see-r and Philip is not. Thus Nathanael can represent the members of the evangelist's own circle of believers,[53] while Philip does not. It is, after all, Nathanael whom Jesus calls "an Israelite indeed."

---

[52]See ch. 1 above, pp. 14–18.

[53]John Painter contends that "there is no evidence that John regards Nathanael as the true Israelite and therefore as the model of the true Israel [believers]. . . . Rather he is really a blunt and guileless Israelite." See J. Painter, "Christ and the Church in John 1, 45-51," in M. de Jonge, ed., *L'Evangile de Jean: Sources, rédaction, théologie* (Bibliotheca Ephemeridum Theologicarum Lovaniensium, 44; Louvain: University Press, 1977) 360. In my judgment it is Painter's position for which there is little evidence.

7

Epilogue

Nathanael, the community's and the evangelist's "true Israelite," appears again in the epilogue to the Fourth Gospel, where "Nathanael of Cana in Galilee" is numbered among the disciples gathered together on the shore of the Sea of Tiberias. Nothing further is said about him, but presumably he is one of Simon Peter's companions when the group of disciples sets out on their fishing expedition.

The epilogue to the Gospel concludes with a verse that might well have been placed at the very end of the New Testament: "But there are also many other things which Jesus did; were every one of them to be written, I suppose that the world itself could not contain the books that would be written" (John 21:25).

These sentiments are very much mine as I come to the conclusion of this short study on the Fourth Gospel. I have chosen to call the book *John and His Witness*. It is about a man named John, called by God to bear witness. As his role is portrayed in the Fourth Gospel, John has no function in life other than to bear witness. In this respect the evangelist's characterization of John is consistent indeed.

Bearing witness to the Christ, John leads two of his disciples to Jesus. One of them, Andrew, bears witness to Christ and so leads his brother Simon Peter to Christ. There is a chain of witnessing to Christ, which bears the testimony to him across the generations and ultimately down to the evangelist's own times. In this way, the evangelist shares with his readers his understanding of the transmission of the faith and the nature of discipleship.

Although the chain of human testimony to the Christ is an integral element in the call to discipleship, the call is ultimately an invitation by Christ to come and see. In what appears to be a set of new beginnings (John 1:43),[1] the evangelist dwells on the theme of the invitation as he portrays Christ first calling Philip in the classic fashion and then promising Nathanael, called to be a see-r, a vision of the Son of Man in glory.

Notwithstanding the evangelist's new beginnings in John 1:43, there is a clearly discernable line in his narrative development. With the first interrogation he raised the messianic issue (John 1:20). With the promise of the vision of the Son of Man he brings his narrative to its climax. The vision of the Son of Man in glory is the manifestation of the Christ.

The evangelist's repeated use of "the next day" allows him to focus on different aspects of his theme. He announces his theme as "the testimony of John" (John 1:19) and provides that testimony in negative form on day one of his narrative schema. "The next day" (John 1:29), he presents his testimony in positive form. "The next day" (John 1:35), he portrays the effect of the testimony. Then, on "the next day" (John 1:43), he describes the ultimate effects of the testimony that is borne to Jesus.

The reader of the Gospel is certainly by now aware that the evangelist's narrative functions on a twofold level. There is the level of his narrative development and the significant level to which his symbols can only point. For this reason I have chosen to title this book *John and His Witness,* a title that likewise functions on two levels. On a narrative level, "John" is the one known to Christian tradition as "the Baptist" and the one esteemed by the evangelist as the witness. "Witness" is the testimony of John, its contents, and its effects.

On another level, "John" is the author of the Gospel, an anonymous person whom many generations of Christians have confused with one of the Twelve, John the son of Zebedee. His "witness" is the testimony that he has borne to Jesus by means of a marvelously dramatic tale of those first Christian witnesses.

---

[1] I am not convinced by H. H. Kuhn's argument that v. 43 is an insertion into the text. See H. H. Kuhn, "Joh 1, 35-51—Literarkritik und Form" *Trier Theologische Zeitschrift* 96 (1987) 149-155.

Throughout this book I have chosen to call the author of the Gospel "the evangelist." The choice of terminology was not without intent. There was a pragmatic reason for my choice. I did not want to confuse the readers with too many Johns. My restriction of the name "John"[2] to John the witness has allowed me to carefully distinguish between the author and the one about whom he is writing.

There was, however, another reason for my choosing to write about "the evangelist." That is my conviction, shared with the vast majority of biblical scholars today, that John, the son of Zebedee, did not write the Fourth Gospel. The Gospel was written by an anonymous author toward the end of the first century. One of the first Christian authors to call the author "John" was Irenaeus (d. ca. 177), the bishop of Lyons. He wrote: "John, the disciple of the Lord, he who had leaned on his breast, also published the Gospel, while living at Ephesus in Asia." Contemporary scholarship has clearly demonstrated that Irenaeus' reflections were based on a legendary view designed to bear witness to the apostolic origins of the Gospel text. Despite the legendary origins of that tradition, "John" has continued to serve as a convenient symbol with which to designate the author of the Gospel. I might also have done so, had I not been concerned to carefully distinguish the evangelist from John the witness.

To write about the work of the evangelist also required some discipline on my part. The literary history of the Fourth Gospel is a complicated history indeed. Contemporary biblical scholars frequently write about what might be called the "different editions" of the Fourth Gospel as they describe its literary development and its different literary strata. Some of these scholars talk about various documents lying behind the Fourth Gospel, specifically about a "signs source," which might have provided the evangelist with source material for John 1:35- 51. Certainly the epilogue (John 21) seems to have been appended to a more-or-

---

[2]When using such technical terms as the "Johannine circle" or "the Johannine 'we,' " I felt it necessary to depart from my self-imposed restriction. Nonetheless I have tried to limit the departures from the rule to a minimum.

less final form of the Gospel by another hand.[3] To write simply about "the evangelist" as I have done is to pass over these complex questions of the literary origins of the Fourth Gospel, with regard to which contemporary scholarship is engaged in a vigorous debate.

Notwithstanding the complexities of the matters but heartened by a remark made by the late and great British scholar C. H. Dodd, I have chosen to use "the evangelist" as an umbrella term to cover all those who have contributed in a literary fashion to the Gospel as it has been passed along to us. In his inimitable manner Dodd wrote: "I conceive it to be the duty of an interpreter at least to see what can be done with the document as it has come down to us before attempting to improve upon it."[4] When he wrote those words, Dodd was reflecting on the work of scholars such as Bultmann, who were so convinced that the traditional version of the Fourth Gospel was the final result of a complex literary process that they attempted to reconstitute its penultimate, and presumably purer, state before beginning the real interpretation of the Gospel.

Such exegetical *tours de force* are part of the history of the interpretation of the Fourth Gospel. To the extent that they are only part of history, they limit the pertinence of Dodd's remarks to a given moment in exegetical history. Nonetheless his remarks do remain pertinent even today. There is some advantage to be had in interpreting the Fourth Gospel as it presently exists. Literary critics remind us that it is a text, no matter how that text has come into being. I have attempted to treat of the Fourth Gospel as an extant text. Thus I have used "the evangelist" as a symbolic expression to designate all of those authors responsible for the present literary existence of the Fourth Gospel.

The evangelist concludes his work with a remark about the many other things that could be written and the many books that

---

[3] Note the apparent conclusion of the Gospel in John 20:30-31. J. K. Thornecroft has suggested that the "two others of his disciples" in John 21:2 are the author of the Gospel and the author of John 21. Cf. J. K. Thronecraft, "The Redactor and the 'Beloved' in John," *Expository Times* 98 (1987) 135-39.

[4] C. H. Dodd, *The Interpretation of the Fourth Gospel* (Cambridge: University Press, 1953) 290.

would be needed for the narration of those untold realities. As I conclude this book, I am likewise convinced that many other things could have been written. However, the series in which it appears, named after the one short of stature (Luke 19:3), required that brevity be a hallmark of the work.

Not only have I limited this study of the Fourth Gospel to John and his witness using John 1:19-51 as the principal focus, I have also tried to be more than circumspect in my footnoted references. Although the modern world is large enough to contain all the books that have been written on the Fourth Gospel, any bibliographer must recognize that the collection is vast.[5] For the past seventy years, the rate of publication on the Fourth Gospel has been approximately a book a week. If one were to add to this collection of books the various articles that have been written, one would have to recognize that a good-sized library would be required to contain the literature on the Gospel.

Just prior to the epilogue the evangelist writes, "Now Jesus did many other signs in the presence of the disciples, which are not written in this book" (John 20:30-31). Let my colleagues in the field of Johannine studies not be offended by the fact that so many other things, including their names—for I am well aware of my indebtedness to them—are not written in this book. Let the reader be aware that so much more could have been said even about John 1:19-51, especially with regard to its Christology. Finally, let one and all realize that this study has but a limited focus. That focus is John and his witness.

The story can perhaps best be summed up by saying that disciples need other disciples in order to become disciples. The disciple who has written this book has certainly needed—and benefited—from the witness of other disciples. It is recognition of this fact and in grateful appreciation of their witness that this book is dedicated to J. K., through whom the Father has indeed sustained a life-giving vision.

---

[5]See especially Edward Malatesta, *St. John's Gospel 1920-1965: A Cumulative and Classified Bibliography of Books and Periodical Literature on the Fourth Gospel* (Analecta Biblica, 32; Rome: Pontifical Biblical Institute, 1967) and Gilbert Van Belle, *Johannine Bibliography 1966-1985: A Cumulative Bibliography on the Fourth Gospel* (Bibliotheca Ephemeridum Theologicarum Lovaniensium, 82; Louvain: University Press, 1988).

Bibliography

Barrett, C. K. *The Gospel According to St. John: An Introduction with Commentary and Notes on the Greek Text,* 2nd. ed. Philadelphia: Westminster, 1978.

Brown, Raymond E. *The Gospel According to John.* 2 vols. Anchor Bible, 29, 29A. Garden City, N.Y.: Doubleday, 1966, 1970.

Brown, Raymond E. *The Community of the Beloved Disciple: The Life, Loves, and Hates of an Individual Church in New Testament Times.* New York/Ramsey/Toronto: Paulist, 1979.

Collins, Raymond F. *These Things Have Been Written: Studies on the Fourth Gospel.* Louvain Theological and Pastoral Monographs, 2. Louvain: Peeters, 1990.

Cullmann, Oscar. *The Johannine Circle.* Philadelphia: Fortress, 1976.

Culpepper, R. Alan. *Anatomy of the Fourth Gospel: A Study in Literary Design.* New Testament Foundations and Facets. Philadelphia: Fortress, 1983.

Haenchen, Ernst. *John.* 2 vols. Hermeneia. Philadelphia: Fortress, 1984.

Lindars, Barnabas. *The Gospel of John.* New Century Bible. Greenwood, S.C.: Attic, 1977.

Martyn, J. Louis. *History and Theology in the Fourth Gospel.* 2nd ed. Nashville: Abingdon, 1979.

Moloney, Francis J. "From Cana to Cana (Jn. 2:1–4:54) and the Fourth Evangelist's Concept of Correct and (Incorrect) Faith" *Salesianum* 40 (1978) 817–843.

Schnackenburg, Rudolf. *The Gospel According to St John*. 3 vols. New York: Crossroad, 1987.

Scripture Index

OLD TESTAMENT

NEW TESTAMENT

Names Index

Aaron 62, 84
Abraham 58, 93, 94
Andrew 38, 41, 46–55, 56, 57, 60, 72, 79, 81, 83, 98
Aristotle 32
Bar-Jesus 59
Barabbas 59
Barnabas 59
Barrett, C. K. 47, 103
Barsabbas 59
Bartholomew 59, 81, 86–87
Bartimaeus 59
Beloved Disciple 68–74, 78
Bernard, J. H. 83
Beutler, J. 15
Billerbeck, P. 90
Boismard, M.-E. 14, 30, 47, 62, 72, 80
Borgen, P. 42
Braun, F.-M. 25
Brown, R. E. 18, 20, 47, 55, 76, 87, 103
Brueggemann, W. 16
Bultmann, R. 45, 78, 101
Carson, D. A. 82
Collins, R. F. 23, 24, 25, 28, 34, 35, 38, 40, 41, 42, 52, 53, 63, 65, 69, 73, 96, 103
Crossan, J. D. 71
Cullmann, O. 18, 20, 103
Culpepper, R. A. 52, 63, 70, 82, 85, 103
David 11
de Goedt, M. 28
de Jonge, M. 40, 97
Dodd, C. H. 101
Donfried, K. P. 76
Elijah 11, 12, 13
Ezekiel 24
Forster, E. M. 74
Gamaliel 16, 17

Geoltrain, P. 25
Gnilka, J. 90
Haenchen, E. 23, 47, 103
Hahn, F. 90
Heise, J. 43
Hosea 24
Irenaeus 100
Isaiah 24, 93, 94
Jacob 58, 93, 96
James 46
Jeremiah 24
John, son of Zebedee 46–47, 99, 100
John, the Witness 9–32, 34, 36, 37, 38, 98–99
Joseph 80, 86
Judas 59, 63, 64–68
Justin Martyr 13, 29
Kuhn, H. H. 99
Lamouille, A. 14
Lazarus 26
Leroy, H. 82
Levi, R. 17
Lindars, B. 47, 103
Malachi 11
Malatesta, E. 102
Malchus 66
Malina, B. J. 42
Markah 11
Martha 91
Martyn, J. L. 17, 103
Mary Magdalene 50, 70
Maynard, A. H. 63
Micah 89
Mollat, D. 82
Moloney, F. J. 91, 92, 104
Moses 11, 12, 80, 84, 95
Nathanael 27, 33, 47, 49, 50, 79, 80, 82, 84, 86–97, 98, 99

111